8 Steps
for Developing
Khushū in Salah

Suhaib Sirajudin

Shield Crest

ISBN 978-1-910176-92-4

MMXV

A CIP catalogue record for this book
is available from the British Library

Published by
ShieldCrest
Aylesbury, Buckinghamshire, HP22 5RR
England
www.shieldcrest.co.uk

Table of Contents

Glossary

A'shūra	10th of Muharram
Akhlaq	Manner/Character
Alhumdulillah	All praise is for Allah
Allahu akbar	Allah is the greatest
Ameen	O Allah, accept my Du'a
Asr	Afternoon Prayer (third of five daily prayers)
Ayah	Verse
Badr	Battle of Badr
Dhikr	Remembrance of Allah
Du'a	Supplication
Fajr	Morning Prayer
Fiqh	Islamic jurisprudence
Fuqahā	Scholars of jurisprudence
Hadith	Sayings of the Prophet ﷺ
Haram	Forbidden
Ibadah	Worship
Iman	Faith
Imam	The one who is leading the prayers
Iqama	Second call to prayer
Isha	Night prayer (fifth of five daily prayers)
Istighfar	Asking forgiveness from Allah
Janazah	Funeral
Jibreel	Angel Gabriel
Jinns	Creatures made of smokeless fire
Junub	In a state of impurity following sexual activity
Ka'abah	House of Allah
Khanzab	Special Shaitan appointed for Salah
Khushū'	Being mindful of Allah
Maghrib	Fourth of five daily prayers
Makrūh	Disliked
Maliki	One of the four schools of thought
Masjid (pl Masajid)	Mosque (the whole complex)

i

Miswak (also Siwaak)	Tooth stick for cleaning teeth
Muharram	The first month of the year in the Islamic calendar.
Mustahab	Recommended action (opposite of Makruh)
Qiblah	Direction of the Ka'abah
Quran	Book of Allah
Raan	Sins and evil deeds that cover the heart
Rak'ah	Portion of the Salah
Ramadhan	The ninth month of the year in the Islamic calendar.
Ruku'	Bowing down in the standing position whilst praying
Sahaba	Companion of the Prophet ﷺ
Sajdah	Prostration
Salaf	Ancestor: specifically, a Muslim from the first three generations of the righteous predecessors
Salah	Prayer
Shaitan	Satan
Shari'ah	Legal system of Islam
Shisha	Hookah, nargileh, water pipe for smoking tobacco
Siwaak	Tooth stick for cleaning teeth
Subhan Allah	Glory be to Allah
Sujud	Prostration
Sunnah	The way of the Prophet Muhammad ﷺ
Sunni	A follower of Prophet Muhammad ﷺ and his companions.
Surah	Chapter
Tabi'in	Followers of the Prophet (pbuh) who were contemporaries of the Sahaba
Tajweed	Rules governing pronunciation during recitation of the Qur'an
Takbeer	Saying Allahu Akbar
Taraweeh	Extra night prayers during Ramadan

Tasbih	Saying Subhan Allah
Tashahhud	Last portion of Salah
Tawheed	Oneness of Allah
Wudhu	Ablution
Zuhr	Second of five daily prayers

Introduction

All praise is due to Allah. We praise Him, seek His help, ask His forgiveness, and we repent unto Him. We seek refuge in Allah from the evils of our souls and from our negative deeds. Indeed, whoever Allah guides, none can misguide, and whoever He misguides, there is none that can guide him. I bear witness and testify that there is no deity worthy of worship except Allah, all glory unto Him, and I bear witness and testify that Muhammad ﷺ is His final Messenger, and His perfect worshipper.

Thereafter; Verily, Allah showers us with so many blessings day and night, that we cannot count these blessings. If we were to thank Allah in prostration for the rest of our lives for the eyesight He has given to us, for just this one of His blessings, it would still not suffice as an act of gratitude to Him, and this is by no means an exaggeration. Let us suppose that Allah were to take away your eyesight: even if all the doctors and surgeons in the world were to gather, endeavouring to recover your sight, they would not be able to return Allah's blessing of eyesight.

Allah does not ask much from us. In fact He has only made Salah compulsory upon us five times a day, which although it is an immense blessing in itself, does not come anywhere near to the totality of the blessings of Allah. Yet, when we stand before Allah in Salah, instead of having Khushū', many of us are distracted by Shaitan's whispers and other diversions in our Salah. As a result, by the time we finish our Salah, we have not benefited from its fruits because we had no Khushū'.

Dear readers, if you do not pay immediate attention to the development of Khushū' in your Salah, then when will you acquire Khushū'?

People are broadly divided into six categories with reagrds to Khushū'. The first category are those people who try and develop

Khushū' in every Salah they pray. The second category are those people who try and develop Khushū' in some of their Salah. The third category of people are those who try to develop Khushū' once a week, in the Friday prayers. The fourth category of peope are those who become serious in the month of Ramdhan in the Taraweeh prayers. The fifth category are those who only try to develop this Khushū' once a year on the 27th night in the month of Ramdhan. The sixth category are those who don't ever try to develop Khushū' in their life and they leave this world without performing a single Sajdah with Khushū'. I swear by Allah there is no greater loss than the loss of leaving this world without a single Sajdah done with Khushū'.

This book is filled with treasures and beautiful ideas with which you may adorn your Salah. Avail yourself of these treasures and use them every time you stand before Allah, so that your Salah will become – if Allah wills – the coolness of your eyes, and your Salah becomes a Paradise for you before the Paradise of the Hereafter.

In this book I have elaborated a unique threefold approach to the personal development of Khushū' which is a step by step method designed to make it simple for you not only to remove distractions during your Salah, but is also aimed at bringing it to life; because this process will stimulate Khushū' in your Salah if Allah wills. And Khushū' is the essence of worship. Salah without khushū' is like a body without a soul.

This 'Threefold Method' is divided into three phases: Enlightenment, Obstructions and Actions.

'Threefold Method'

Actions comprise a list of eight steps that you need to implement if you want Khushū'. They are represented by the acronym 'PARADISE'. In other words, if you offer Salah by following the steps contained in the word 'PARADISE' then, - if Allah wills -, your Salah will lead you to high rank in Paradise.

Note: Of course no one will be admitted to Paradise solely on account of their deeds, people are granted Paradise only because of the Mercy of Allah.

The pearls and treasures in this book are the result of my research which I did becaue I my self wanted to develop Khushū' in my Salah. It was March 2014 when I began to worry about distractions in my Salah. I wanted someone to help me towards a Salah with Khushū' and without distractions. I began to search for different ways to improve my Khushū'. This book is the result of that research: the treasures and pearls that were a means and an incentive for me on the way to my journey. I am sharing them with you so that they can be of similar benefit to you in your desire to enhance the level of Khushū' in your Salah.

The steps outlined in this book are easy, simple, straight to the point, and since they worked for me, I can assure you that by following these steps they will work for you too. If Allah wills, the advice and steps that I share with you in these pages can make a huge difference in your Salah. Your Salah will protect you from committing sins. Your Salah will become for you the coolness of your eyes. Your Salah will provide you with peace of mind, warmth in your heart and joy for your soul.

This book will take you through the 'Threefold Method' and the '8 Steps for developing Khushū' in Salah'. It will teach you how to put each step into practice. It will teach you step-by-step how best to accomplish each phase, so that you too can gain the fruits of Khushū' by putting these treasures into practice. Continue to read, and begin to put these steps into practice so that you too can immediately find greater pleasure in Salah.

'8 Steps of Actions'

8 Steps for developing Khushū' in Salah

P — **Preparation**

A — **Awareness**

R — **Recitation**

A — **Arabic**

D — **Dua**

I — **Imagination**

S — **Stance**

E — **Eternal Life**

I pray that that this work will help you come closer to Allah, by realising your own great poverty and helplessness and by appreciating the Beneficence and Generosity of Allah.

S. Sirajudin.

Suhaib Sirajudin
Bolton, UK
10 Rabi al-awal 1436 A.H.

Problems You Could Be Facing

Distractions in Your Salah

This book is probably in your hands because when you are praying Salah you are being distracted. This means that your heart is outside of Salah, though your body is not. You may be praying the whole Salah with your heart and mind engaged in and distracted by worldly matters. This is a serious problem because if you do not do anything about the distractions that you are probably facing in your Salah, by the end of your life it is possible that you have not performed a single Salah with Khushū'! There is no greater loss than that of leaving this world having not performed a single Salah with Khushū'.

On the other hand, if you follow the steps that I am going to share with you in this book, when you are standing in Salah you will feel as though you are standing in front of Allah. You will not be worried about worldly matters and your heart will be full of peace and tranquillity, which will lead you to feel the sweetness of worship in your Salah.

No Effect upon Recitation

Perhaps your problem is that your eyes do not shed tears when you are reciting the Quran.

If, when you are standing before the Almighty, your Creator, Allah Most Merciful and Compassionate, your eyes do not shed tears, when then will they shed tears? Allah revealed the best of speech, the Quran, the book which if it was revealed on a mountain, that mountain would fall down into utter ruin. If your eyes do not shed tears reciting such a powerful book then when will they shed tears?

On the other hand if you do not shed tears whilst reciting the Quran, this may well mean that you are only partially focused on your recitation, so your Salah may not prevent you from sins. And if you continue praying your Salah in this manner, you are losing out on the sweetness of the recitation which you can only appreciate after experiencing it.

Where you want to be is shedding tears whilst reciting the Quran. When you recite the verses of Hell you ask Allah to protect and save you from Hell. When you recite the verses of Paradise you ask Allah to grant you Paradise. When you recite the verses that talk about the things we need to do, you ask Allah to give you the ability to act upon them. When reciting the verses of prohibition, you ask Allah to save you from ignoring them. When you recite the Quran with such Khushū', your Salah will be a means for a positive change in your life. Which means that your Salah may well save you from committing sins and evil acts.

Is Salah Becoming A Burden To You?

Maybe you are reading this book because you are praying Salah just to get it off your shoulder. You experience Salah as a weight on your shoulders, and you just pray it to get rid of the burden. As a result, you begin your Salah towards the end of the allotted prayer time. If this becomes your habit, you could miss your Salah because the time has expired. What a tragedy!

However, by following the steps in this book, you will find the pleasure of standing in front of Allah: Salah will no longer be a burden for you. You will begin looking forward to standing before Him again in your next Salah.

So: you are possibly experiencing these problems in your Salah. Whether you are distracted, you do not shed tears whilst reciting the Quran, or Salah is a burden on your shoulders, you can, - if Allah wills -, develop your Khushū'. The only question is, how do you get from where you are to where you want to be? Well, that's what I would like to share with you in this book: how you can minimise distractions and shed tears when you recite the Quran and get these results in your Salah.

Overview of the Book

The 'Threefold Method' is a system designed for people who want to develop Khushū' in their Salah. This is a three phase system, and taking this approach will help you to develop Khushū'. The three phases are: Enlightenment, Obstructions and Actions. These are the core concepts for developing Khushū' in your Salah. If any of these are missing then the system will not be as effective.

This is not a sequence you must follow: you do not need to be perfect in Enlightenment before you move onto Obstructions, or need to be perfect in Obstructions before you move onto Actions. If you wait to become perfect in one area before moving onto the next one you will never reach the second phase! We as human beings are not creatures of perfection: we have our shortcomings and, therefore, we need to develop Khushū' gradually. I am not suggesting that you put yourself in isolation for several years until you fully develop a phase before moving on to the second or third.

The diagram on the next page is a visual representation of the three phases for developing Khushū' and will be used throughout this book as we explore each one in detail. Each section of the system will be highlighted as it is introduced.

Enlightenment

This is the first phase of the 'Threefold Method'. The content of this phase may not necessarily be something to act upon, but it will be covering core knowledge that will aid you in the overall development of Khushū'. These core elements include the benefits of Khushū', signs of Khushū' and the stories of the Prophet ﷺ, his companions, the pious predecessors and the scholars.

Obstructions

This is the second phase of the system for the development of

Khushū'. Obstructions are those things that act as barriers, stopping you from developing Khushū'. This section is very important, because when you aren't aware of what is stopping you from developing Khushū' in your Salah, then you aren't concerned about getting rid of it. Very often these things exist but we don't pay any attention to them. However, these things are acting as a barrier and an obstruction between you and the development of Khushū' in your Salah. And until you get rid of these obstructions you will not develop Khushū'.

Actions

When you get rid of these obstructions, it will make your path easy to the third phase of the system, the Actions.

Actions are those things that you must do. This is a list of tips and techniques which the people of Khushū' are doing in their Salah. They will be discussed in detail in this section of the book.

Actions is broken down into 8 steps. Doing them will give you pleasure in standing before Allah. The acronym for these steps is 'PARADISE'. In other words, when you perform Salah by following these 8 steps then your Salah will increase your ranks in Paradise by the mercy of Allah.

'Threefold Method'

'8 Steps of Actions'

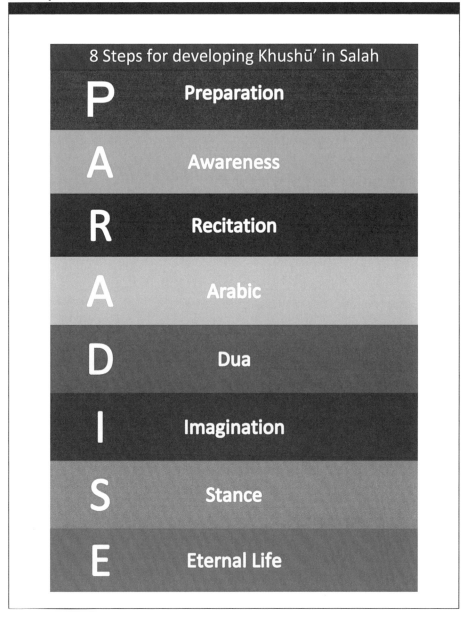

8 Steps for developing Khushū' in Salah

P	Preparation
A	Awareness
R	Recitation
A	Arabic
D	Dua
I	Imagination
S	Stance
E	Eternal Life

These steps will be covered in detail as they are introduced in subsequent chapters.

Our Guarantee

Firstly, guidance is in the hands of Allah. Secondly, this method does not guarantee the development of Khushū' straight away. It is a slow and gradual process and it may take some time, hard work, dedication and effort. Anything you want requires time and effort, so why would you not want to put hard work into perfecting your Salah? If you follow the three phases in this system, I can guarantee you, by the mercy and the will of Allah, that your Salah can be on a higher level, and it can become the coolness of your eyes. It will start giving you the fruits of Salah where you enjoy standing before Allah and you will not feel it a burden on your shoulders to be standing before Him. You will look forward to the next Salah so that you can once again experience the same or, in fact, even more of the sweetness of your Salah.

The reason why I can give you a guarantee that this system will work is simply because all the people who do have Khushū' in their Salah, did exactly what I am going to share with you in this book. The scholars, both of the past and those of today, who have Khushū' in their Salah, followed the same steps that I will be sharing with you. So if it worked for them, why wouldn't it work for you?

The biggest Obstacles preventing Khushū'

When I started to share this system for developing Khushū' with people, I came across three major obstacles preventing people from implementing this method. If you are not aware of these obstacles, you might not realize that they can be overcome. This book is intended to help you past these difficulties so that you gain the pleasure of Salah instead of remaining where you are.

Misconception – You Must Be A Scholar

The biggest obstacle that I discovered is that people think they cannot develop Khushū'. Some people genuinely believe only a scholar can truly develop Khushū'.

It is true that you cannot develop Khushū' in your Salah to equal the Khushū' of the Prophet ﷺ, but that does not mean you cannot develop Khushū' at all. Khushū' can be developed by anyone to a very high level at which you will enjoy your Salah, you will experience the sweetness of worship, and when you prostrate to Allah, you will not want to raise your head from prostration.

As to the idea that you have to be a scholar, I do not believe this to be necessary. Two things, however, are. The first – and more important – of them is the mercy of Allah. If you need anything, then you will get it through the mercy of Allah. Without the mercy of Allah, all the tips and techniques I will share with you will prove fruitless.

The second thing that is required is knowledge. You can be a student of knowledge and have Khushū' without being a single-minded scholar. What is important is that you have the relevant knowledge. If there is no knowledge, then how would you recognise the advice and methods for developing Khushū'? So, the right knowledge is required for any one to develop Khushū'.

I don't have a Mentor

To some extent, having a mentor is important. In fact, it carries many benefits. It reduces the feeling of isolation, it gives you better understanding, and it provides experience which you may not get from only reading a book. However, keeping this in mind, I have broken the whole process down into simple, easy to follow phases and steps that are intended to produce a sense of belonging to the people with Khushū', which helps to counteract any feeling of isolation.

I don't have enough time

This is one of the most common obstacles that I have found amongst people; they often claim they don't have the time. I have just one response to this claim: 'If you don't have time now, then when will you have time?' If you are not going to take time out today to improve your Salah, when will you take this time out? Do you not know that Salah is the central pillar of Islam, which means that if it is not well founded then the stability of the entire religion is compromised?

So, dear reader, take time out to develop Khushū' in your Salah, and do not allow this fallacy to dissuade you from travelling the road to attaining it. This obstacle is nothing more than a whisper from the Shaitan.

You have been chosen by Allah

The reason why you have this book in your hands is because you have been guided to be here. Allah has guided you and you have been chosen by Allah to improve your Salah. You are concerned about Khushū' in your Salah, and the only reason for this is that Allah has chosen you and guided you to come closer to Him by developing Khushū' in your Salah. Since you have been chosen by Allah, thank Allah for His mercy upon you, for choosing you out of the billions of people in the world.

You can do it too

I was quite recently in the same position as you. In early 2014 I started to worry about my Salah. I would pray Salah and I would be distracted. Sometimes, I would feel that my heart was not at peace even after praying Salah. So, I started searching for the means to develop Khushū' in Salah, because I knew that it was the lack of Khushū that was causing these problems.

I read books and listened to tapes and cds on this topic. As I discovered tips and techniques that could develop Khushū' in Salah, I began putting them into practice, and this helped me greatly in the development of Khushū' in my Salah.

I then shared these tips and techniques with my students and other people around me who were in a similar situation to mine, and here is what one of them had to say:

"Easy, simple, step by step and most of all, a powerful system that has helped me with Khushū' in my Salah from the very first day." (Abdullah)

In this book, I am only sharing with you the tips because I found them useful. By putting them into practice, I can assure you, - if Allah wills -, they will help you in the way they helped me. If you follow the steps in this book, you will taste the fruits of Salah in this world, and you will be amongst the successful ones. If you don't follow these steps then you will remain where you are, continuing to be distracted in your Salah. You will continue to have a recitation in Salah that is merely recitation and not a recitation of pondering and reflection. Your Salah will continue to feel like a burden on your shoulders. If you do not take action to combat these problems, you will end up being amongst the losers. Losers merely take information without acting upon it: successful people take the information and follow it to get closer to Allah. May Allah include you and me amongst the successful ones. Ameen.

How to use this Book

Before we begin with the 'Threefold Method', I want to make two important points which, if taken seriously from the outset, will greatly increase the benefit you will obtain from this material.

Firstly, I would recommend that you do not see this material as a 'book'. What do I mean by this? Well, people are aware of the importance of self-development, so they go and buy a book, read it once and put it away. I call this 'shelf-development' rather than 'self-development'. Have you ever considered that your library knows more than you do?

You may choose to read this material once through completely for a sense of the whole, but my recommendation to you is to treat this material as a personal companion in the continual process of change and growth. Try to put each point into practice as you study, and focus on each one as it arises throughout the process.

As you progress to deeper levels of understanding and implementation, you can return repeatedly to the previous steps and work to expand your knowledge and actions.

Secondly, I would suggest that you move your frame of mind from that of a learner to that of a teacher. What do I mean? When you come to each step, besides you yourself following it through and benefiting from it, try to share it with others, starting with your loved ones and those close to you. Start with your spouse, your children and reach out to the people around you. You probably know people who are stressed, worried, or in difficulty. It is more than likely that Salah with Khushū' is part of the solution for their stress and troubles. Allah tells us in the Quran:

"Verily, in the remembrance of Allah do hearts find rest"
(Quran [3] 13:28)

Authenticity

Finally, there is no better way by which we can learn how to develop Khushū' than the method given to us by Allah our Creator, and His last and final Messenger, Prophet Muhammad ﷺ. Therefore, throughout the process, we will stick to methods found in the Quran and the Hadith, which will give you confidence in the authenticity of the steps you will be taking on your path to the development of Khushū'.

ENLIGHTENMENT

The Meaning of Khushū'

Khushū', linguistically, means lowering, humbling and calmness. It is to be humble in front of Allah. It also means serenity, tranqu

illity and dignity.

Khushū' also means that the heart stands before Allah in humility and submission. (Madarij Salikeen)

Allah uses this word in the Quran:

$$وَخَشَعَتِ الْأَصْوَاتُ لِلرَّحْمَنِ$$

All voices will be humbled for the Most Gracious (Allah), (Quran [3] 20:108)

Khushū' is to submit your heart in the presence of Allah, by lowering and humbling it. Khushū' is the essence of worship. The more you have Khushū' in your Salah, the greater the reward. An act of worship without Khushū' is like a body without a soul. When you offer Salah without Khushū' then it remains merely posturing and empty gestures without intrinsic value to them. When the Quran is recited without Khushū' it has no effect. Similarly, when Salah is prayed without Khushū' it has no effect.

Khushū' is developed in the heart and the results of it manifest on the body. This brings to mind the hadith of the Prophet ﷺ who said: "Beware! There is a piece of flesh in the body, if it becomes good (reformed), the whole body becomes good, but if it gets spoilt, the whole body gets spoilt and that is the heart." (Bukhari)

Fruits of Khushū'

Please find a place to read these next few pages where you can be alone and uninterrupted. Clear your mind of everything except what you will read and what I will invite you to do. Don't worry about your schedule, your business, your studies, your family, or your friends. Just focus with me and open your mind completely. This is about your Hereafter, the day on which you will be standing before Allah. The first account that will be taken on the day of Judgement will be that of your Salah. You **CANNOT** afford not to pay attention.

In your mind's eye, imagine you have never driven a car before, and you are starting to learn how to drive. Am I right in thinking that you will not embark on learning to drive before you know the benefits of driving a car? When you realize that by being able to drive, you will be able to get from A to B much faster than you can now.

This is how the human mind works: when we don't know the benefits of something we tend to ignore it, or not pay attention to it. This phase of the 'Threefold Method' will educate you as to the fruits of having Khushū' in your Salah. You will see the amazing benefits that you are missing out on by not having Khushū' in your Salah, and your desire to gain greater Khushū' will help you in your studies.

Khushū' – a Characteristic of the Prophets

Khushū' is a characteristic of the Prophets and the Messengers. Allah talks about the character of Zakariya ﷺ:

$$\text{وَزَكَرِيَّا إِذْ نَادَىٰ رَبَّهُ رَبِّ لَا تَذَرْنِي فَرْدًا وَأَنْتَ خَيْرُ الْوَارِثِينَ}$$

And (remember) Zakariya, when he cried to his Lord: "O my Lord! leave me not without offspring, though Thou art the best of inheritors. (Quran [1] 21:89)

Ponder and reflect over this verse of the Quran. Who is Allah talking about? Allah is talking about one of the prophets whose name is Zakariya ﷺ. What did Zakariya ﷺ do? What was his state at the time of making this Du'a? He called upon Allah. He was in

3

the state of Du'a, in the state of worship, and Du'a requires Khushū'. He was alone and no one saw him besides Allah. What did he say? He said: "O my Lord! Leave me not without offspring, though Thou art the best of inheritors." When this Du'a came out from the heart of Zakariya ﷺ with Khushū', his Du'a was answered immediately. How?

فَاسْتَجَبْنَا لَهُ وَوَهَبْنَا لَهُ يَحْيَىٰ وَأَصْلَحْنَا لَهُ زَوْجَهُ

So We listened to him: and We granted him Yahya: We cured his wife's (barrenness) for him. (Quran [1] 21:90)

What did Zakariya ﷺ ask of Allah? He asked Allah to bless him with offspring. He made this Du'a with Khushū'. How did Allah respond? What did Allah grant him? When Allah gives, He gives more than what you ask for, because He is Generous. Allah cured his wife's barrenness, and the child born was Yahya, another Prophet. This was more than he had asked for, it was a separate gift from Allah. When you have Khushū' in your Salah, Allah will give you more than what you ask for.

Khushū' – a Characteristic of the Scholars

Khushū' is a characteristic of the scholars. Allah says:

إِنَّ الَّذِينَ أُوتُوا الْعِلْمَ مِن قَبْلِهِ إِذَا يُتْلَىٰ عَلَيْهِمْ يَخِرُّونَ لِلْأَذْقَانِ سُجَّدًا - وَيَقُولُونَ سُبْحَانَ رَبِّنَا إِن كَانَ وَعْدُ رَبِّنَا لَمَفْعُولًا - وَيَخِرُّونَ لِلْأَذْقَانِ يَبْكُونَ وَيَزِيدُهُمْ خُشُوعًا

Those who were given knowledge beforehand, when it is recited to them, fall down on their faces in humble prostration"
And say: "Glory to our Lord! Truly has the promise of our Lord been fulfilled!"
They fall down on their faces in tears, and it increases their (earnest) humility. (Quran [1] 17:107–9)

Khushū' – a Characteristic of the Believers

Khushū' is a characteristic of the believers. Allah says:

قَدْ أَفْلَحَ الْمُؤْمِنُونَ – الَّذِينَ هُمْ فِي صَلَاتِهِمْ خَاشِعُونَ

Successful indeed are the believers. [2]
Those who humble themselves in their prayers; [1]
(Quran 23:1-2)

Believers have Khushū' at all times, especially during Salah as these verses of the Quran describe. A believer's heart turns humble when the Quran is being recited. His heart turns humble when he enters Salah. His heart turns humble when he sees the signs of Allah, which remind him of Allah.

Belivers also have Khushū' outside of Salah, for instance, when the weather is hot, the believer humbles himself, because extreme heat reminds him of the heat of Hell. In winter when the weather is cold, the cold weather reminds the believer of the coldness of the Hell. When the believer sees the moon, he humbles himself, because the moon reminds the believer of Paradise and the seeing Allah in Paradise. "You shall see your Lord in the Hereafter as you are seeing this moon: and you will not feel the slightest discomfort in seeing Him." (Bukhari and Muslim). When Ramadhan comes, again the believer humbles himself, because the month of Ramadhan reminds the believer of Paradise: "the gates of Paradise are open and the gates of Hell are closed." (Bukhari)

Khushū' will give you Peace in the final moments of your Life

So the believer is constantly in Khushū' in different stages of his life. He is constantly moving from one stage of Khushū' to another stage of Khushū', until he reaches his last moments when Allah grants him peace of heart, after a long journey of Khushū'. This peace of heart is only given after developing Khushū'. Allah says in

5

the Quran:

$$\text{أَلَمْ يَأْنِ لِلَّذِينَ آمَنُوا أَنْ تَخْشَعَ قُلُوبُهُمْ لِذِكْرِ اللَّهِ وَمَا نَزَلَ مِنَ الْحَقِّ}$$

Has not the time arrived for the Believers that their hearts in all humility should engage in the remembrance of Allah and of the Truth which has been revealed (to them),
(Quran [1] 57:16)

$$\text{أَلَا بِذِكْرِ اللَّهِ تَطْمَئِنُّ الْقُلُوبُ}$$

Verily, in the remembrance of Allah do hearts find rest (peace)" (Quran [3] 13:28)

In other words, you will not gain peace in your heart when you lack Khushū'. When your heart humbles itself and it has Khushū', Allah will give your heart peace. And when your heart is at peace, then Allah will purify your soul. Allah says:

$$\text{قَدْ أَفْلَحَ مَنْ زَكَّاهَا – وَقَدْ خَابَ مَنْ دَسَّاهَا}$$

Truly he succeeds that purifies it, And he fails that corrupts it! (Quran [1] 91:9-10)

Khushū' is the main characteristic of the Prophets, it is the main characteristic of the scholars, and that of the believers. This whole book is about developing Khushū' so that when you arrive at the final moments in your life, you will leave this world with peace of heart and a purified soul. The true value of a peaceful heart and a purified soul will only be realized when a person leaves this world and he is in the next life.

Of course, developing Khushū' is a long slow process, but your journey will be accelerated if you follow the pearls and treasures shared with you in this book.

One Sajdah of Khushū' will remove all your worries and anxieties

Many of us have worldly problems, it is very ordinary to suffer from anxieties and worries. For most of us, even during our Salah, these worldly problems and worries do not leave us. This can mean that we finish our entire Salah still in the emotional state we were in before commencing the Salah.

Amongst the benefits that you will gain by having Khushū' in Salah is that it will remove all of the worldly worries and anxieties that you may be experiencing. Try to do one Sajdah with Khushū', crying, and see how you feel. Try it, and by Allah, one Sajdah of Khushū' will remove all of the worries and anxieties that you could be suffering in your daily life. Do you ever remember doing a Sajdah with Khushū' and weeping that when you raised your head your heart was without peace?

If you carried the worries and anxieties of the entire world, if you were overwhelmed with debts, and you did just one Sajdah with Khushū', all of these worries and anxieties would come to an end with this one Sajdah. By Allah, one Sajdah with Khushū' gives peace to your heart, because Khushū' is the key to peace. That is why the Prophet ﷺ, said:

جعلت قرة عيني في الصلاة

The coolness of my eyes lies in Salah (Ahmed, Nasai)

Khushū' will give you success in both Worlds

Success is what we all want, and it is exactly what you will get if you have Khushū'. Allah says in the Quran, describing the believers:

قَدْ أَفْلَحَ الْمُؤْمِنُونَ – الَّذِينَ هُمْ فِي صَلَاتِهِمْ خَاشِعُونَ

Successful indeed are the believers [2].

7

Those who humble themselves in their prayers [1];
(Quran 23:1-2)

Success is a very general term, and the reason why Allah did not make it specific, is because the success referred to in this verse is comprehensive success, success in this world and in the Hereafter.

Khushū' will increase your sustenance

One of the reasons why we don't have Khushū' and we get distracted in our Salah is because of the busy life that we all lead: the life of work, study, business, social life, life online in Facebook and WhatsApp, and so on. The moment we start our Salah we are just waiting to finish it so that we can go back to our social life, our business and work.

What you don't perhaps realize is that Allah is the One Who provides for us, He is the One Who sustains us: having Khushū' in your Salah is a means of increase in your sustenance. You may ask, how is that possible? How can Khushū' in Salah increase my sustenance? What has Khushū' in Salah got to do with sustenance? You must increase your belief and trust in Allah. Have this trust in Allah, believe that Allah is truly the One Who will increase your sustenance if you have Khushū' in Salah, and you will see results.

When Zakariya ﷺ called upon Allah, with humility and Khushū', Allah gave him Yahya ﷺ and on top of that Allah cured his wife's barrenness and made his son a prophet. So when you have Khushū' it will increase in your sustenance. Don't you want increase in your sustenance? Develop Khushū' and see the increase of sustenance from Allah as a gift to you.

Khushū' will increase your reward

Allah says in the Quran that He has prepared forgiveness and a great reward for the men and women who have Khushū':

وَالْخَاشِعِينَ وَالْخَاشِعَاتِ وَالْمُتَصَدِّقِينَ وَالْمُتَصَدِّقَاتِ وَالصَّائِمِينَ
وَالصَّائِمَاتِ وَالْحَافِظِينَ فُرُوجَهُمْ وَالْحَافِظَاتِ وَالذَّاكِرِينَ اللَّهَ كَثِيرًا
وَالذَّاكِرَاتِ أَعَدَّ اللَّهُ لَهُمْ مَغْفِرَةً وَأَجْرًا عَظِيمًا

......for men and women who humble themselves, for men and women who give in charity, for men and women who fast (and deny themselves) for men and women who guard their chastity and for men and women who engage much in Allah's praise — for them has Allah prepared forgiveness and great reward. (Quran [1] 33:35)

The Prophet ﷺ said in a long Hadith after mentioning the virtues of ablution:

فَإِنْ هُوَ قَامَ فَصَلَّى فَحَمِدَ اللَّهَ وَأَثْنَى عَلَيْهِ وَمَجَّدَهُ بِالَّذِي هُوَ أَهْلٌ
لَهُ وَفَرَّغَ قَلْبَهُ لِلَّهِ إِلاَّ انْصَرَفَ مِنْ خَطِيئَتِهِ كَهَيْئَتِهِ يَوْمَ وَلَدَتْهُ أُمُّهُ

"if he stands to pray and praises Allah, lauds Him and glorifies Him with what becomes Him and shows wholehearted devotion to Allah, his sins would depart leaving him (as innocent) as he was on the day his mother bore him." (Muslim)

On one occasion, Uthman ؓ after performing a complete ablution said that the Prophet ﷺ said:

مَنْ تَوَضَّأَ نَحْوَ وُضُوئِي هَذَا ثُمَّ قَامَ فَرَكَعَ رَكْعَتَيْنِ لاَ يُحَدِّثُ فِيهِمَا
نَفْسَهُ غُفِرَ لَهُ مَا تَقَدَّمَ مِنْ ذَنْبِهِ

He who performs ablution like this ablution of mine and then stands up (for prayer) and offers two rak'ahs of prayer without allowing his thoughts to be distracted, all his previous sins are expiated. (Bukhari and Muslim)

In these pearls of the Prophet ﷺ the people of Khushū' are

9

rewarded with a gift of forgiveness and a great reward from the King of all kings, the One Who is the most merciful and the One Who gives without any limits.

Khushū' causes the Descent of Angels

Do you know that when you read Quran, the angels descend, and they listen to your recitation? On one occasion, Usaid ibn Hudair ﷺ, was reciting Surah Baqarah at night and his horse was suddenly startled and troubled. Whenever he stopped reciting, the horse would become quiet. Every time he began to recite, the horse would become agitated, and would become quiet again every time he stopped. Usaid ﷺ said, "When I looked at the sky, I saw something like a cloud containing what looked like lamps." In the morning when Usaid ﷺ related this to the Prophet ﷺ, he said: "Do you know what that was?" Ibn Hudair replied, "No." The Prophet ﷺ said:

$$\text{تِلْكَ الْمَلَائِكَةُ دَنَتْ لِصَوْتِكَ وَلَوْ قَرَأْتَ لَأَصْبَحَتْ يَنْظُرُ النَّاسُ إِلَيْهَا لَا تَتَوَارَى مِنْهُمْ}$$

"Those were Angels who came near to you for your voice and if you had kept on reciting till dawn, they would have remained there till morning when people would have seen them as they would not have disappeared." (Bukhari)

When you recite the Quran in your Salah, and your mind is wandering and is lacking Khushū', imagine how many blessings you are losing out on. When angels descend, Allah's mercy descends. What more could you wish for than the mercy of Allah? His mercy is better than the world and everything it contains.

Khushū' will make your Salah easy for you

We all know the importance and the obligation of Salah, yet for

10

Enlightenment

many of us, when the time comes for Salah, whether we are at work, or at college or in our businesses, we tend to delay it. We may not necessarily delay it outside of its time, but for most of us, especially for those living busy lives in the West, Salah is not performed at the beginning of its time.

Salah, for some of us, is viewed as an obstruction or interruption: something in our way. You are preoccupied by your business, but your Salah disrupts your business or your work. There are also people who treat Salah as something they just need to get over and done with. These attitudes result from the lack of Khushū' in the Salah, so you treat it as a burden on your shoulders. Allah says, talking about Salah in the Quran:

$$وَإِنَّهَا لَكَبِيرَةٌ إِلَّا عَلَى الْخَاشِعِينَ$$

It is indeed hard, except to those who are humble. (Quran
[1] 2: 45)

When you have Khushū' in your Salah, your Salah will become easy for you. You will be looking forward to the time for the next Salah, so that you can gain the pleasure of the coolness of your eyes in Salah, just as the Prophet ﷺ found the coolness of his eyes in Salah.

So if you have Khushū' in your Salah, your Salah will become easy for you and it will not be difficult or a burden for you.

Khushū' in Salah will keep you away from sins

$$إِنَّ الصَّلَاةَ تَنْهَىٰ عَنِ الْفَحْشَاءِ وَالْمُنْكَرِ$$

For Prayer restrains from shameful and unjust deeds
(Quran [1] 29:45)

Have you ever wondered why it is that although you pray Salah, it does not keep you away from evil and sins? This is a common question asked by many people. Imagine someone who has diabetes, and goes to a doctor. The doctor prescribes some medication, adding that it will only work alongside a controlled diet. Of course, if the patient chooses to do nothing about their diet, then there can be no justifiable complaint about the failure of the medication.

Salah is prescribed by Allah to keep a person away from committing sins as long as the Salah is prayed with Khushū'. In the same way that the medication for diabetes will not work with the wrong kind of diet, similarly if the Salah is prayed without Khushū', it will not keep you away from committing sins.

A man came to the Prophet ﷺ and said:

إِنَّ فُلَاناً يُصَلِّي الليل كلَّه، فإذا أصبح سرق، فقال: سِينْهَاه ما تقول،

أو قال: ستمنعه صلاته

So and so prays at night, but in the morning he steals. He said: What you mention concerning him will make him give it up; or He said: His Salah will make him give it up. (Musnad Ahmed)

Therefore, if you pray Salah with Khushū, with consciousness of the recitation then your Salah will keep you away from committing sins.

Khushū' leads to Shedding Tears

If your eyes do not shed tears whilst standing before Allah, then when else will they shed tears? The main reason why eyes don't shed tears is because of lack of Khushū' in Salah. The more khushū' you have in your Salah, the more your eyes will shed tears. These tears that you shed in your Salah are valuable but you will only realize their true value in the Hereafter. You will ask Allah to send you back to this world so that you can shed a tear, but it will be too late.

حَتَّىٰ إِذَا جَاءَ أَحَدَهُمُ الْمَوْتُ قَالَ رَبِّ ارْجِعُونِ – لَعَلِّي أَعْمَلُ صَالِحًا فِيمَا تَرَكْتُ

When death comes to one of them, he says: "O my Lord! Send me back (to life) In order that I may work righteousness in the things I neglected."
(Quran [1] 23:99-100)

Pay close attention to what the Prophet ﷺ said regarding the tears that you shed. Look at the value of a tear that is shed for the sake of Allah. The Prophet ﷺ said:

لاَ يَلِجُ النَّارَ رَجُلٌ بَكَى مِنْ خَشْيَةِ اللهِ حَتَّى يَعُودَ اللَّبَنُ في الضَّرْع

"A man who weeps for fear of Allah will not enter Hell until the milk goes back into the udder." (Tirmidhi)

He further said:

لَيْسَ شَيْءٌ أَحَبَّ إِلَى اللَّهِ مِنْ قَطْرَتَيْنِ قَطْرَةٌ مِنْ دُمُوعٍ مِنْ خَشْيَةِ اللَّهِ، وَقَطْرَةُ دَمٍ تُهَرَاقُ فِي سَبِيلِ اللَّهِ

"There is nothing more beloved to Allah than two drops: A tear shed due to fear of Allah, and a drop of blood spilled in the path of Allah." (Tirmidhi)

He further said:

عَيْنَانِ لَا تَمَسُّهُمَا النَّارُ: عَيْنٌ بَكَتْ مِنْ خَشْيَةِ اللَّهِ، وَعَيْنٌ بَاتَتْ تَحْرُسُ فِي سَبِيلِ اللَّهِ

"There are two eyes which the fire of hell will not touch: One is the eye that cried out of the fear of Allah and (the other is) an eye which spent the night on watch in the cause of Allah." (Tirmidhi)

Such is the value of a tear that you shed for the sake of Allah. A time will come very soon (Hereafter) when you will shed tears of blood but they will have no value. The value of tears is in this world, shed them before Allah, only for His sake, and I pray that Allah may include you and me amongst those who are entitled to His reward. Ameen.

The question remains: How do I shed these tears? What are the steps that will help me get to this point? This will be covered in the third section of the 'Threefold Method', where I will describe to you the Actions required to arrive at this level - if Allah wills -.

Khushū' will make standing on the Day of Judgement easier

Ibn Qayyim (رحمة الله عليه) says:

"A slave stands in front of Allah on two occasions. The first during Salah and secondly on the Day of Judgment. Whosoever stands correctly in the first, the second standing will be made easier for him. And whosoever disregards the first standing, the second standing will be extremely difficult." (Ibn Qayyim, Al – Fawaid, P.435)

وَمِنَ اللَّيْلِ فَاسْجُدْ لَهُ وَسَبِّحْهُ لَيْلًا طَوِيلًا – إِنَّ هَؤُلَاءِ يُحِبُّونَ الْعَاجِلَةَ
وَيَذَرُونَ وَرَاءَهُمْ يَوْمًا ثَقِيلًا

And part of the night, prostrate thyself to Him; and glorify Him a long night through.
As to these (disbelievers), they love the fleeting life, and put away behind them a Day (that will be) hard.
(Quran [1] 76:26-27)

Khushū' will enhance your reflection upon the Quran

Imagine if you were to offer your Salah behind an Imam who prays and recites the Quran with a beautiful voice, but he has no Khushū'; compare this with an Imam who recites the Quran with

Khushū', who sheds tears as he recites. Which of them will help you ponder over its meanings (presuming you understand the Quran)? It will be the one who recites the Quran with Khushū' and who cries whilst reciting the Quran.

So when there is Khushū' in Salah, and in your recitation of the Quran, it will help you towards deeper reflection upon the recitation of the Quran. This could mean that since you are reflecting upon the Quran, you will benefit from the guidance given to you by Allah, which could mean that eventually your Salah will keep you away from evil and sins, which is one of the purposes of offering Salah.

Khushū' will give you coolness of the eyes

Praying Salah with Khushū' will give you coolness of the eyes. This same Salah provided coolness of eyes for the Prophet ﷺ, who said:

جعلت قرة عيني في الصلاة

The coolness of my eyes lies in Salah (Ahmed, Nasai)

The Khushū' of the Prophet ﷺ

If you wanted to make a million dollars, wouldn't you look at someone who has already made a million dollars and learn the tips and techniques from him so that you too can follow his example? You most probably would. If you would do this for the prize of a million dollar, then what about Khushū', which is priceless? The value of Khushū' is beyond a million dollar. In order to develop Khushū', it only makes sense that we take the tips from the one who had the most Khushū' and the greatest fear of Allah i.e. the Prophet ﷺ. This section also recounts the descriptions of the Khushū' of the Companions and the Pious Predecessors.

These descriptions of Khushū' are mentioned here not so that we read them as stories, but to soften our hearts and to help us to emulate them. True, we may never reach their level, but we should aim high so that even if we miss the target, we will be closer to it than had we not raised our sights in the first place.

Allah tells us in the Quran,

> "Observe patience, as the resolute messengers observed patience" (Quran [2] 46:35)

Now, can we ever have patience like the messengers of Allah? No, we cannot even come close to their patience, but yet Allah is telling us to take that level of patience as our goal; for although our goal is unattainable, when we aim so high, whatever we achieve will be higher than we ever thought possible. Therefore, when reading these stories, take this level of Khushū' as your goal.

Description of the Weeping of the Prophet ﷺ

Abdullah ibn ash-Shikh-kheer ؓ narrates:

أتيت رسول الله صلى الله عليه وسلم وهو يُصلِّي ولصدره أَزِيزٌ كأزيز

16

المِرجل من البكاءِ

"I saw the Messenger of Allah ﷺ praying, and I heard the sound of his weeping coming out of his chest, which was like the sound of a boiling pot." (Abu Dawood)

The Prophet ﷺ wept for different reasons. Sometimes he wept due to his fear and concern for his nation. Sometimes he wept due to the fear of Allah; he also wept when listening to the Quran.

Tears of the Prophet ﷺ due to the fear of Allah

قال بلال: يا رسول الله لِمَ تبكي وقد غفر الله لك ما تقدّم من ذنبك وما تأخر، قال: "أفلا أكون عبداً شكوراً، لقد نزلت عليّ الليلة آية، ويل لمن قرأها ولم يتفكر فيها: إِنَّ فِي خَلْقِ السَّمَوَاتِ وَالْأَرْضِ وَاخْتِلَافِ اللَّيْلِ وَالنَّهَارِ لَآيَاتٍ لِأُولِي الْأَلْبَابِ

Bilaal ؓ asked, "O Messenger of Allah, why do you weep when Allah has forgiven you all your past and future sins?" He said, "Should I not be a grateful slave? Tonight some verses have been revealed to me; woe to the one who recites them and does not think about what is in them: 'Behold! In the creation of the heavens and the earth, and the alternation of Night and Day, there are indeed Signs for men of understanding.' " (Ibn Hibban)

Tears of the Prophet ﷺ whilst listening to the Quran

عن عبد الله بن مسعود رضي الله عنه قال: قال لي رسول الله صلى الله عليه وسلم: "اقرأ عليّ القرآن" فقلت: يا رسول الله! أقرأ عليك؛ وعليك أُنزل؟ فقال: "نعم، فإني أُحبُّ أن أسمعه من غيري" قال ابن مسعود: فقرأت عليه سورة النساء فلما بلغت: (فَكَيْفَ إِذَا جِئْنَا مِنْ كُلِّ أُمَّةٍ بِشَهِيدٍ وَجِئْنَا بِكَ عَلَى هَؤُلَاءِ شَهِيداً)، قال : "حسبك الآن"

فالتفت إليه فإذا عيناه تذرفان

Ibn Mas'ūd ؓ reported: The Prophet ﷺ said to me, "Recite the Quran to me." I said: "O Messenger of Allah! Shall I recite it to you when it was revealed to you?" He said, "I like to hear it from others." Then I began to recite Surah An-nisa. When I reached the verse: 'How will it be when We shall bring a witness from every people and bring you as a witness against them?' (Having heard it) he said, "Enough! Enough!" When I looked at him, I found his eyes were overflowing with tears. (Bukhari and Muslim)

Tears of the Prophet ﷺ in Salah

عن علي بن أبي طالب رضي الله عنه، قال: ما كان فينا فارس يوم بدرٍ غير المقداد، ولقد رأيتنا وما فينا إلا نائم إلا رسول الله صلى الله عليه وسلم تحت شجرةٍ يُصلّي ويبكي حتى أصبح

Ali ؓ said, "Only Al-Miqdad had a horse during Badr, and at some point, I found that all of us had fallen asleep, except the Messenger of Allah. He was praying under a tree and wept until dawn. (Ahmed)

Tears of the Prophet ﷺ in the Salah of Solar Eclipse

عن عبد الله بن عمرو رَضِيَ اللهُ عَنْهُ قال: انكسفتِ الشمس يوماً على عهد رسول الله صلى الله عليه وسلم، فقام رسول الله صلى الله عليه وسلم يُصلّي، ثم سجد، فلم يكد يرفع رأسه، فجعل ينفخ ويبكي، ويقول رب لم تعدني هذا وأنا فيهم لم تعدني هذا وأنا أستغفرك وذكر الحديث، وقال: فقام فحمد الله وأثنى عليه، وقال: "عُرِضَتْ عليَّ النار فجعلت أنفخها، فخفت أن تغشاكم"

18

Abdullah ibn Amr ؓ narrates, "The sun eclipsed during the time of the Prophet ﷺ. The Prophet ﷺ got up to pray, then he prostrated, and he was not going to raise his head. He started gasping and weeping, saying: 'O my Lord, did You not tell me that You would not do that while I was still among them? Did You not tell me that You would not do that while we are asking You for forgiveness?' The Prophet ﷺ stood and praised and glorified Allah and said, 'Hell was brought so near to me that I tried to ward it off for fear it may overwhelm you.' " (Nasai)

Tears of the Prophet ﷺ due to his Compassion for his Nation

عن عبد الله بن عمرو رَضِيَ اللهُ عَنْهُمَا: أنّ النبيَّ صلى الله عليه وسلم تلا قول الله عز وجل في إبراهيم: ﴿رَبِّ إِنَّهُنَّ أَضْلَلْنَ كَثِيراً مِنَ النَّاسِ فَمَنْ تَبِعَنِي فَإِنَّهُ مِنِّي﴾ الآية، وقال عيسى عليه السلام: ﴿إِنْ تُعَذِّبْهُمْ فَإِنَّهُمْ عِبَادُكَ وَإِنْ تَغْفِرْ لَهُمْ فَإِنَّكَ أَنْتَ الْعَزِيزُ الْحَكِيمُ﴾ الآية، فرفع يديه وقال: "اللهم أُمَّتي أُمَّتي" وبكى، فقال الله عز وجل: "يا جبريل اذهب إلى محمد وربُّك أعلم فسله ما يُبكيك؟ فأتاه جبريل عليه السلام فسأله، فأخبره رسول الله صلى الله عليه وسلم بما قال وهو أعلم، فقال الله: يا جبريل! اذهب إلى محمد فقل: إنَّا سَنُرضيك في أُمَّتك ولا نسوؤك"

Abd-Allah ibn 'Amr ؓ said: The Prophet ﷺ recited the verse about Ibrahim ؑ; "O my Lord! They have indeed led astray many among mankind. But whosoever follows me, he verily, is of me." (Quran [3] 14:36); and the verse in which 'Esa ؑ said, "If You punish them, they are Your slaves, and if You forgive them, verily, You, only You are the Almighty, the All-Wise." (Quran [3] 5:118). Then he raised his hands and said: "O Allah, my nation, my nation." Allah said: "O Jibreel, go to Muhammad, although your Lord knows best, and ask him why he is weeping." So Jibreel went to him and asked him, and the Messenger of Allah ﷺ answered him, although He knows best. Allah said: "O Jibreel, go to Muhammad and say: "I will make you pleased concerning your nation and not displeased." (Muslim)

The Khushū' of the Companions

The Companions of the Prophet ﷺ would follow the Prophet ﷺ in the Khushū' of their Salah.

Khushū' of Abu Bakr ﷺ

عَنْ عائشة رَضِيَ اللهُ عَنْهَا قالت: لَمَّا ثَقُلَ رَسُولُ اللَّهِ صلى الله عليه وسلم جَاءَ بِلَالٌ يُؤذِنُهُ بِالصَّلَاةِ، فَقَالَ: "مُرُوا أَبَا بَكْرٍ فَلْيُصَلِّ بِالنَّاسِ"، فَقُلْتُ: يَا رَسُولَ اللَّهِ، إِنَّ أَبَا بَكْرٍ رَجُلٌ أَسِيفٌ، وَإِنَّهُ مَتَى يَقُمْ مَقَامَكَ لَا يُسْمِعُ النَّاسَ، فَلَوْ أَمَرْتَ عُمَرَ؟ فَقَالَ: "مُرُوا أَبَا بَكْرٍ فَلْيُصَلِّ بِالنَّاسِ" وفي رواية: قالت عائشة: إِنَّ أَبَا بَكْرٍ إِذَا قَامَ مَقَامَكَ لم يُسْمِعِ النَّاسَ مِنَ الْبُكَاءِ، فَمُرْ عُمَرَ فَلْيُصَلِّ بِالنَّاسِ

Aisha ﷺ said: When the Prophet ﷺ became seriously ill, Bilal ﷺ came to him for the prayer. "Tell Abu Bakr to lead the people in prayer." I said to him, "Abu Bakr is a softhearted man and if he stands in your place, he would not be able to make the people hear him. Will you order Umar ﷺ to lead the prayer?" The Prophet ﷺ said: "Tell Abu Bakr to lead the people in prayer." (According to another narration) Aisha ﷺ said: "If Abu Bakr stands in your place, the people would not hear him owing to his (excessive) weeping. So please order 'Umar to lead the prayer." (Bukhari and Muslim)

Khushū' of Umar ﷺ

كان أمير المؤمنين عمر بن الخطاب رضي الله عنه يصلي بالناس صلاة الفجر، فطعنه أبو لؤلؤة المجوسي، فقال عمر حين رأى نزف الدماء: قولوا لعبد الرحمن بن عوف فليصلِّ بالناس، ثم غُشي على عمر رضي الله عنه، فحُمل فأدخلوه بيته، فلمَّا أفاق، قال: "أصلَّى

الناس؟" قالوا: نعم، فقال: "لا إسلام لمن ترك الصلاة"، ثم دعا

بوضوء فتوضأ، ثم صلَّى، ثم أمر بعد صلاته من يسأل عن من قتله؟

فأخبروه أنه طعنه أبو لؤلؤة

Umar ﷺ was leading the people in Fajr prayer. Abu Lu'lu the Zoroastrian stabbed him. Umar ﷺ upon seeing the bloodshed, said: "Tell Abdurrahman ibn Awf to lead the prayer." Umar ﷺ fell unconscious, so they picked him up and took him home. After Umar ﷺ regained consciousness, the first thing he asked was, "Have the people prayed?" And they informed him, "Yes!" He said, "There is no Islam for the person who disregards prayer." He asked for water to perform Wudhu, he performed Wudhu and offered his Salah. He then asked who had stabbed him, and they informed him it was Abu Lu'lu. (Manaqib Umar, Ibn Jawzi)

The first thing he asked after he became conscious was, "Have the people prayed?" which shows he was more concerned for the Salah than for his own self. Further, he prayed his own Salah before asking who had stabbed him, showing that he was more concerned about the Salah than knowing who had stabbed him.

Khushū' of S'ad Ibn Mu'adh ﷺ

عن سعد بن معاذ أنه قال: "فيَّ ثلاث خصال لو كنت في سائر

أحوالي أكون فيهن كنت أنا أنا: إذا كنت في الصلاة لا أُحَدِّثُ

نفسي بغير ما أنا فيه، وإذا سمعت من رسول الله صلى الله عليه وسلم

حديثاً لا يقع في قلبي ريب أنه الحق، وإذا كنت في جنازة لم أُحَدِّث

نفسي بغير ما تقول ويُقال لها"

S'ad Ibn Mu'adh ﷺ said: "I have three qualities which I wish I could keep up all the time, then I would really be something. When I am praying, I do not think about anything except the prayer I am doing; if I hear any hadith from the Prophet ﷺ I do not have any doubts about it; and when I attend a Janazah (funeral), I do not think about anything except what the Janazah says and what is said in response to it." (Majmooul Fatawa of Ibn Taymiyyah)

The Khushū' of Abdullah Ibn Zubair ؓ

عبد الله بن الزبير كان يسجد فأتى المنجنيق فأخذ طائفة من ثوبه وهو في الصلاة لا يرفع رأسه

Abdullah Ibn Zubair ؓ was once prostrating when a missile from a catapult was launched at him, and part of his garment was torn away whilst he was praying, but he did not even raise his head. (Majmooul Fatawa of Ibn Taymiyyah)

The Khushū' of Ammar Ibn Yasir ؓ

During the expedition of Dhat Ar Riqa, Abbad ibn Bishr and Ammar ibn Yasir ؓ both volunteered to stay awake at night guarding the Muslims. As Ammar ibn Yasir stood up for Salah, one of the idolaters shot him with an arrow. He (Ammar ibn Yasir) pulled it out. This was repeated three times in succession. He went into Ruku' and Sujud, when Abbad ibn Bishr noticed what had occurred. Abbad ibn Bishr seeing the blood flowing from Ammar ibn Yasir asked him: "Subhan Allah! Why did you not inform me the first time you were shot?" He replied:

كنت في سورة أقرؤها فلم أحب أن أقطعها

"I was reading a Surah, and did not want to stop (reciting)." (Abu Dawood)

The Khushū' of the Tabi'in and the Pious Predecessors

The Companions of the Prophet and the Pious Predecessors were always fearful and afraid to present a prayer to Allah which had no Khushū'. They were filled with fear that their deeds may not be accepted.

The Khushū' of Sufyan Thawree (رحمة الله عليه)

Sufyan Thawree (رحمة الله عليه) was seen in the Haram at the time of the Maghrib prayer, he held such a long prostration, that he did not lift his head until the call for Isha was heard. (Akhbar Salaf Salih)

The Khushū' of Imam Bukhari (رحمة الله عليه)

Imam Bukhari (رحمة الله عليه) said that once whilst praying Salah an insect had bitten him repeatedly. Upon the completion of the prayer, he asked, "Look, what was hurting me in my Salah?" They saw that it was an insect that had bitten him in 17 places and he did not break off his Salah.

According to a narration, this was a voluntary prayer that he was praying after Zuhr Salah.

Imam Bukhari (رحمة الله عليه) was asked, "Why did you not leave your Salah when it bit you the first time?" he replied: "I was reciting a Surah and wished to complete it." (Seyar A'alam Nubla)

Statement of Hasan (رحمة الله عليه)

Al-Hasan, (رحمة الله عليه), said, "When you stand in prayer, stand in due obedience as Allah has ordered you, beware of negligence and looking (here and there), beware that

Allah is looking at you while you are looking at something else, asking Allah for Paradise and taking refuge with Him from the Fire, yet your heart is heedless, not knowing what the tongue is saying." (Bayhaqi)

The Khushū' of Muslim bin Yasaar (رحمة الله عليه)

Muslim bin Yasaar (رحمة الله عليه) was praying in the Masjid when a portion of the building collapsed. He was completely unaware of the event due to his Salah. (Seyar A'alam Nubla)

The Khushū' of Amir Ibn Abdullah (رحمة الله عليه)

'Amir bin Abdullah (رحمة الله عليه) was one of the humble in prayer. He was asked: "Does anything come into your mind in your prayer?" He replied: "Is there something that is more beloved to me than Salah that should come to my mind?" They said: "Verily, things come to our minds when we pray." He said to them: "Such as Paradise and the Maidens of Paradise and thing like this?" They said: "No. Our families and our wealth." 'Amir replied: "I would rather spears pass through my body than get that sort of thing in my prayer."

The Khushū' of one of the Pious Predecessors

A person amongst the pious predecessors was once in need of amputation and was faced with the difficulty of surgery without anaesthesia. He was offered alcohol to help decrease the pain he would undoubtedly feel but he refused saying: "Cut it off while I am in prayer." The amputation was completed while he was in prostration and he didn't feel the pain.

The Khushū' of Habeeb ibn abi Thabit (رحمة الله عليه)

Abu bakr ibn Ayyash (رحمة الله عليه) says about the prostration of Habeeb ibn abi Thabit (رحمة الله عليه) that: "If you were to see him prostrating, you would assume he had passed away, due to the long duration of his prostration."

The Khushū' of Amir Ibn Qays (رحمة الله عليه)

Amir ibn Qays was on the verge of death, he kept weeping. He was asked, "Why do you cry?" He said, "I do not do it for fear of death, nor for caring about life, but I weep for missing the thirst during the hot days [when fasting] and for missing praying at night during winter." (Seyar A'alam Nubla)

Dear Reader! This is what makes them cry. What makes you cry?

A Warning for the one praying Salah without Khushū'

Khushū' is the essence of prayer. A body that has no soul is a dead body, a Salah that has no soul is a dead Salah. Imagine you are the boss of your company, and you want to hire an employee: if a dead body is presented to you would you accept that body? Of course you wouldn't, because that body has no soul. Similarly, when a person prays Salah without Khushū', it is as if he is presenting a dead Salah in the presence of Allah. That's why there are statements in the Quran and the Hadith warning us against praying Salah without khushū'.

Lack of calmness in Salah is considered an Omitted Salah

عن أبي هريرة رضي الله عنه: أن رجلاً دخل المسجد ورسول الله جالس فيه فرد عليه السلام، ثم قال له: ارجع فصل فإنك لم تصل. فرجع فصلى كما صلى، ثم جاء فسلم علي النبي فرد عليه السلام ثم قال: ارجع فصل فإنك لم تصل، فرجع فصلى كما صلى، ثم جاء فسلم على النبي فرد عليه السلام، وقال: ارجع فصل فإنك لم تصل ثلاث مرات، فقال في الثالثة: والذي بعثك بالحق يا رسول الله ما أحسن غيره فعلمني. فقال : إذا قمت إلى الصلاة فكبر، ثم اقرأ ما تيسر معك من القرآن، ثم اركع حتى تطمئن راكعاً، ثم ارفع حتى تعتدل قائماً، ثم اسجد حتى تطمئن ساجداً، ثم اجلس حتى تطمئن جالساً، ثم اسجد حتى تطمئن ساجداً، وافعل ذلك في صلاتك كلها.

Abu Hurayra ﷺ narrates that a person entered the Masjid and performed Salah. The Prophet ﷺ was present in the Masjid at the time. After the person had completed his Salah he came to the Prophet ﷺ and greeted him.

27

The Prophet ﷺ replied to his greeting and then said, "Go back and perform Salah, undoubtedly you have not performed Salah." He went and performed Salah in exactly the same manner as he had done before. He came back to the Prophet ﷺ and greeted the Prophet ﷺ. The Prophet ﷺ replied to his greeting and said, "Go back and perform Salah, you have not performed Salah." He went and performed Salah again in exactly the same manner as he had done before. This happened a third time and after the person had prayed Salah the third time he said, "O Prophet of Allah! By the Lord who sent you with the truth, I cannot pray Salah better than this, please teach me." The Prophet ﷺ said, "When you stand for Salah, say the Takbeer and recite the parts of the Quran which are easy for you. Then bow down until you feel satisfaction, then stand up fully (meaning ensure your back is straight). Then prostrate until you feel satisfaction, then sit calmly and prostrate calmly and perform your whole Salah in such a manner." (Bukhari and Muslim)

A Person could have Prayed for 60 Years without Allah ever having accepted a single one of his Prayers

The Prophet ﷺ said:

إِنَّ الرَّجُلَ لَيُصَلِّي سِتِّينَ سَنَةً، وَمَا تُقْبَلُ لَهُ صَلاَةٌ، لَعَلَّهُ يُتِمُّ الرُّكُوعَ، وَلاَ يُتِمُّ السُّجُودَ، وَيُتِمُّ السُّجُودَ، وَلاَ يُتِمُّ الرُّكُوعَ

"There could be a person who prays for 60 years but his Salah is not accepted, it could be because he completes Ruku' and does not complete Sujud, or he completes Sujud and does not complete Ruku'. (Musannaf ibn abi Shaybah)

28

The worst Thief is the one who steals from his own Prayer

The Prophet ﷺ said:

"أَسْوَأُ النَّاسِ سَرِقَةً الَّذِي يَسْرِقُ مِنْ صَلَاتِهِ" قَالُوا: يَا رَسُولَ اللَّهِ، وَكَيْفَ يَسْرِقُ مِنْ صَلَاتِهِ؟ قَالَ: "لَا يُتِمُّ رُكُوعَهَا وَلَا سُجُودَهَا"

The worst thief is the one who steals from his own prayer. People asked, "Messenger of Allah! How could one steal from his own prayer?" He said: "By not completing its Ruku' and Sujud." (Ahmed)

Allah does not look at the Salah of the one who does not straighten his back between Ruku' and Sajdah

The Prophet ﷺ said:

"لَا يَنْظُرُ اللَّهُ إِلَى صَلَاةِ عَبْدٍ لَا يُقِيمُ فِيهَا صُلْبَهُ بَيْنَ رُكُوعِهَا وَسُجُودِهَا"

"Allah does not look at the Salah of the slave who does not straighten his back between his Ruku' and Sujud. (Ahmed)

A person dying without completing his Ruku' and making short Sajdahs dies upholding a religion other than the Religion of Muhammad ﷺ

The Prophet ﷺ saw a man praying who did not complete his Ruku' and made a very short Sajdah. The Prophet ﷺ said:

لَوْ مَاتَ هَذَا عَلَى حَالِهِ هَذِهِ، مَاتَ عَلَى غَيْرِ مِلَّةِ مُحَمَّدٍ صلى الله عليه وسلم

29

"If this man dies while praying in this manner, he will die upholding a religion other than the religion of Muhammad." (Tabrani)

A man may complete his Salah and only have one-tenth recorded

The Prophet ﷺ said:

إِنَّ الرَّجُلَ لَيَنْصَرِفُ وَمَا كُتِبَ لَهُ إِلَّا عُشْرُ صَلَاتِهِ، تُسْعُهَا، ثُمْنُهَا، سُبْعُهَا، سُدْسُهَا، خُمْسُهَا، رُبْعُهَا، ثُلُثُهَا، نِصْفُهَا

"A man may complete the Salah and only have recorded for himself one-tenth or one-ninth or one-eighth or one-seventh or one-fifth or one-fourth or one-third or one-half." (Abu Dawood)

A man could pray for 40 years and not one Salah is written for him

Huzaifa ؓ entered the Masjid and saw a person performing Salah who was not bowing or prostrating correctly. When he was about to leave, Huzaifa ؓ asked the person, "How long you have been performing Salah in that manner?" The person replied, "For the last forty years." Huzaifa ؓ said:

مَا صَلَّيْتَ مُنْذُ أَرْبَعِينَ سَنَةً، وَلَوْ مِتَّ وَهَذِهِ صَلَاتُكَ لَمِتَّ عَلَى غَيْرِ الْفِطْرَةِ الَّتِي فُطِرَ عَلَيْهَا مُحَمَّدٌ صلى الله عليه وسلم

"You have not performed any Salah in forty years and if you die whilst performing Salah like you just performed, then you will not die on that path of Muhammad ﷺ." (Nasai)

The Prayer of a Hypocrite

The Prophet ﷺ said:

تِلْكَ صَلَاةُ الْمُنَافِقِ يَجْلِسُ يَرْقُبُ الشَّمْسَ حَتَّى إِذَا كَانَتْ بَيْنَ قَرْنَيْ الشَّيْطَانِ قَامَ فَنَقَرَهَا أَرْبَعاً لَا يَذْكُرُ اللَّهَ فِيهَا إِلَّا قَلِيلاً

"The manner of Salah of the hypocrites is that they wait for the sun to set, up to the point that it (the sun) is between the two horns of Shaitan and then they stand (for Salah). He then bangs his head (on the earth) four times and he remembers Allah but rarely." (Muslim)

Signs of Khushū'

Picture with me someone driving a car and as he is driving in heavy traffic, he comes too close to the vehicle in front of him and his front bumper touches the vehicle in front; what do you think he would do? Wouldn't he come out of his car to check the bumper for any scratches? Yes, he would check for signs of damage to the vehicles. These signs tell you the severity of the damage. In the same way, when you offer Salah there are certain signs, and these signs will tell you if you have Khushū' in your Salah or not. The more you have of these signs the more Khushū' you have, and vice versa. Would you like to know these signs? Carry on reading!

Hastening to do Good Deeds

One of the signs Allah gives in the Quran is the sign of hastening towards good deeds. Allah talks about Zakariya ﷺ, his wife and Yahya ﷺ:

$$ إِنَّهُمْ كَانُوا يُسَارِعُونَ فِي الْخَيْرَاتِ $$

They used to hasten on to do good deeds. (Quran [3] 21:90)

A person who has Khushū' is always swift to action: when an opportunity arises to do something good, he is one of the first to do it. Whether it is giving charity, or a time to forgive, he is quick to do so. So the sign of Khushū' that Allah emphasizes the most is that of readiness to do good deeds. Zakariya ﷺ and his family were swift to perform good deeds and Allah described them as people with Khushū'.

This sign of hastening towards good deeds was common amongst the Companions. Many times Abu Bakr and Umar ﷺ would vie with each other in performing good deeds.

Umar ؓ reported: The Prophet ﷺ ordered us to give charity and at the time I possessed some wealth. I said to myself, "If there is a day I can do better than Abu Bakr, then this is the one." So I went with half of my wealth to the Messenger of Allah and he said, "What have you left for your family?" I said, "The same amount." Then Abu Bakr came with everything he had. The Prophet said, "O Abu Bakr, what have you left for your family?" He said, "Allah and His Messenger." I said, "By Allah, I will never do better than Abu Bakr." (Tirmidhi)

So this shows that the Companions and the righteous predecessors would compete with each other and hasten to do good deeds, and this is one of the many signs of Khushū'.

Compete with one another in doing good deeds. The deed does not need to be as big as giving all your wealth, it can be as small as learning a few more verses of the Quran than usual, being the first to volunteer at Islamic events, arriving at the Masjid earlier to sit at the front, praying that Sunnah prayer, or giving more in charity than usual – small actions add up.

Some people dislike the notion of competing with one another. If this competition is for worldly matters, i.e. you are competing in gaining more wealth, or getting a better car than your friend, or a better house than your neighbour, it is not desirable. Competing for the Hereafter is what the Companions and the righteous predecessors did. Allah says:

$$سَابِقُوا إِلَى مَغْفِرَةٍ مِنْ رَبِّكُمْ وَجَنَّةٍ عَرْضُهَا كَعَرْضِ السَّمَاءِ وَالْأَرْضِ أُعِدَّتْ لِلَّذِينَ آمَنُوا بِاللَّهِ وَرُسُلِهِ$$

Compete with each other in proceeding towards forgiveness from your Lord and to Paradise the width of which is like the width of the sky and the earth. It has been prepared for those who believe in Allah and His messengers. (Quran [2] 57:21)

Calling Upon Allah with Hope and Fear

Allah describes another sign of Khushū' in this verse. Referring to Zakariya ﷺ and his family, Allah says:

$$وَيَدْعُونَنَا رَغَبًا وَرَهَبًا ۚ وَكَانُوا لَنَا خَاشِعِينَ$$

And they used to [...] call Us with hope and fear; and they were humble to Us. (Quran [3] 21:90)

Calling upon Allah, making Du'a to Allah, worshipping Allah, performing all acts of good deeds with hope and fear of Allah are all signs of Khushū'. This is because when both Hope and Fear are together in the same heart then the heart remains in a state of Khushū'. When the heart is in a state of Khushū', it brings Khushū' to your eyes, which then brings Khushū' to your face and finally your entire body has Khushū'. Allah says:

$$خُشَّعًا أَبْصَارُهُمْ$$

With their eyes humbled (Quran [2] 54:7a)

If Allah wants He can reject every act of worship that you do. Our deeds are not worthy of acceptance: with the amount of mistakes we make in our deeds, they do not merit acceptance. It is by the mercy of Allah that He accepts our deeds. So the presence of Fear and Hope in your acts of worship demonstrates Khushū'.

Your level of righteousness is better than before

Amongst the signs of Khushū' is that after you have prayed your Salah, you are closer to Allah than you were prior to it. As we mentioned earlier, praying Salah with Khushū' will stop you from committing evil deeds. So if you are closer to Allah than you were prior to this salah then know that this is a sign of Khushū'.

The reason why our Salah does not stop many of us from committing sins, is because our Salah has become simply something that we need to do every day and as long as we have prayed it, we are fine with it. A person who has Khushū' in his Salah, his salah will prevent him from going to the wrong path.

When you are heart broken if you miss a Salah, or you feel uneasy if you miss the first row in the Masjid, or you get distressed by missing a Sunnah in your Salah; when someone feels these things, it shows that this person has inner Khushū'.

Remembering the Hereafter in Abundance

When was the last time you remembered meeting Allah? When was the last time you remembered standing before Allah? When was the last time you remembered you are going to return to Allah? When was the last time you remembered death?

Most of us don't remember death, we don't even like the word death, so we have changed it to 'passing away': so and so has passed away. Dear readers, death is something we need to remind ourselves of constantly and frequently. Death is something that will come to you and me and everyone, and the one who remembers death often, the more he remembers it, the greater his increase in Khushū'. The more you remember meeting Allah, the more you will develop Khushū'. The less you remember meeting Allah, and standing before Him, the less you will develop Khushū'. Allah describes the people of Khushū' in the Quran: who are they? What are their qualities? What are their signs?

الَّذِينَ يَظُنُّونَ أَنَّهُم مُّلَاقُو رَبِّهِمْ وَأَنَّهُمْ إِلَيْهِ رَاجِعُونَ

Who bear in mind the certainty that they are to meet their Lord, and that they are to return to Him. (Quran 2: [1] 46)

Remember that you are going to meet Allah and that you will stand before Him one day.

35

Humbling and prolonging your Prostration

One of the signs of Khushū' is to prolong your prostration. The more you prolong your prostration, the more you will gain Khushū' in your Salah. The one who prostrates in a hasty manner and does not prolong his prostration, the less he has Khushū' in his Salah.

Khushū' is the opposite of pride and arrogance. Khushū' is humbling yourself in the presence of Allah. You will never find a person who has Khushū' with pride and arrogance. The further away a person is from pride, the closer he is to Khushū' and the closer a person is to pride the further away he is from Khushū'. Pride, arrogance, and Khushū' are totally incompatible.

The eyes of a proud person do not shed tears, because his heart does not have Khushū'. A person with pride and arrogance does not prolong his prostration, he prostrates in a hasty manner. Iblees was told to prostrate, but he didn't prostrate because of pride and arrogance. Therefore prolong your prostration and don't lift your head up in a hasty manner. Allah says about the disbelievers of Makkah:

وَإِذَا قِيلَ لَهُمُ اسْجُدُوا لِلرَّحْمَنِ قَالُوا وَمَا الرَّحْمَنُ أَنَسْجُدُ لِمَا تَأْمُرُنَا وَزَادَهُمْ نُفُورًا

And when it is said to them, "Prostrate yourselves to the Rahman (the All-Merciful, Allah)," they say "What is Rahman? Shall we prostrate ourselves to the one to whom you direct us?" And it increases nothing in them except aversion.
(Quran [2] 25:60)

The Facial Signs of Khushū'

The scholars have mentioned that one of the signs that you may see on a person who has Khushū' are tears flowing from the eyes

36

while the face smiles. You may ask, how can they both go together, tears and smiling? It seems rather contradictory. Tears flow due to Khushū' and fear of Allah, and smiling is due to the peace that is felt in the heart.

> Do you remember the feeling you may have had at the time when the Quran was completed in the month of Ramdhan? How did you feel after that long Du'a? Did you not cry or feel like crying during this Du'a? Didn't you feel peace in your heart after this Du'a? That peace that you felt, that tranquillity, that serenity, is the peace that is felt after you gain Khushū'. (Shinqitee)

These are the signs of Khushū', and the more Khushū' there is, the more these signs will appear upon an individual. You may be asking, well, how do I attain these signs? It is simply by doing what the people of Khushū' would do and not doing what they wouldn't do. The next two sections will teach you these actions so that you will be on your way to developing Khushū' in your Salah.

OBSTRUCTIONS

Obstructions

This is the second phase for developing Khushū'. Obstructions are those things that act as a barrier and prevent you from developing this Khushū'. This section is very important because, when you are not aware of the things that are stopping you from developing Khushū' in your Salah, you will make no effort to remove them. Many times, these obstructions are there but we sometimes just don't notice them, while, in fact, these obstructions are acting as a barrier between you and Khushū' in your Salah; and so long as you do not protect yourself from these obstructions, they will continue preventing you from developing Khushū' in your Salah.

Sins – the Greatest Obstacles to Khushū'

Sins are the greatest obstacle in your development of Khushū'. Sins act as a barrier between a person and Khushū' in Salah. The reason for this is because sins prevent the mercy of Allah. Khushū' in Salah is a mercy from Allah, so when sins intrude between a person and the mercy of Allah, it prevents a person from gaining Khushū' in his Salah. That's why the Prophet ﷺ would begin his Salah with the following Du'a:

اللَّهُمَّ بَاعِدْ بَيْنِي وَبَيْنَ خَطَايَاىَ كَمَا بَاعَدْتَ بَيْنَ الْمَشْرِقِ وَالْمَغْرِبِ، اللَّهُمَّ نَقِّنِي مِنَ الْخَطَايَا كَمَا يُنَقَّى الثَّوْبُ الأَبْيَضُ مِنَ الدَّنَسِ، اللَّهُمَّ اغْسِلْ خَطَايَاىَ بِالْمَاءِ وَالثَّلْجِ وَالْبَرَدِ

O Allah! Set me apart from my sins (faults) as the East and West are set apart from each other and clean me from sins as a white garment is cleaned of dirt (after thorough washing). O Allah! Wash off my sins with water, snow and hail. (Bukhari)

This shows that sins act as a barrier between a person and his

39

Khushū' in Salah, so the Prophet ﷺ would ask Allah to separate him from them as the East and West are set apart from each other.

Scholars say, never look at the size of the sin, instead look at who you have disobeyed. Don't look at the fact that the sin is minor and therefore, it is ok for you to do it, because it's only minor. Never think light of any disobedience because, at the end of the day, the disobedience is to Allah, and therefore it makes no difference whether the sin is minor or major.

Strategies for Abstaining from Sins

Many of us fall into disobeying Allah day and night. I think some of us end up blaming Shaitan, that it was Shaitan who caused me to commit this act, it was Shaitan who led me to this. But remember: Shaitan has no power other than the power of whispering. His only weapon is that of whispering and he cando no more than that. This being the only power he has, we cannot really blame Shaitan for every sin that we commit.

Therefore, the Quran and the Hadith give us some steps and if you follow them, besides helping you to stay far away from sins, you will get closer to Allah.

First Strategy – Allah's Help

The first step, which is the most important step of all that will help you to stay away from sins, is the help of Allah. You can follow all the strategies to help you abstain from sins but if His help is not there, then following all the tips and techniques I am going to share with you will not help.

The way to attain the help of Allah is by making Du'a to Him to help you stay far away from disobedience. The Prophet ﷺ would make Du'a to Allah in his Salah, asking Allah to help him stay away from sins.

Make Du'a to Allah in abundance and say, 'O Allah, keep me away from sins, O Allah do not make me close to sins, O Allah instead of sins, make me do righteous deeds.' Make Du'a to Allah, because Du'a is the essence of worship, and there is no better place to make Du'a than in your Salah.

So Du'a is the first step to take that will help to keep you away from sins: make Du'a to Allah and ask Him to keep you far away from His disobedience.

Second Strategy – Knowing Allah

Imagine with me that you are an employee of a company. One day your boss approaches you and tells you that today he is going to monitor your performance at work. He is going to monitor your breaks, your work and everything related to your work. Wouldn't you make sure that your work is up to a high standard? Of course you would, and the reason is because you know that your boss is going to monitor your performance today. Awareness of your boss and knowing that he is going to monitor you will increase your level of performance and decrease your shortcomings.

The reason why sins are committed is because those who sin are not aware of who Allah is. They don't have the knowledge of Allah: the more knowledge of Allah a person has the further away he will be from sins, and the further away he is from sins then, naturally, the closer he will be to Allah.

If a person is contemplating a sin, and at that moment he remembers just one fragment of his knowledge of Allah, he would instantly say, 'I fear Allah' and he would restrain himself.

The way to get this knowledge of Allah, is by studying 'Tawheed – Oneness of Allah'. You may refer to my book on this subject, 'Master Tawheed In 24 Hours'. This book will teach you the knowledge of your Creator, Allah. There is no better knowledge to acquire than the knowledge of knowing Allah.

Obstructions

The second step in increasing the knowledge of Allah is by reading the Quran, pondering over the Quran, reading the commentaries of the Quran, sitting in the study gatherings of the Quran and the Hadith. When you do these righteous actions, this will increase your knowledge of Allah, and the moment you are faced with a sin, your heart will cry out and say 'I fear Allah' and you will restrain yourself.

Third Strategy – The Consequences of Sins

When you drive a car, you know that if you were to break the speed limits you could cause an accident, which could damage your car and possibly hurt yourself. Doesn't this knowledge lead you to stay within the speed limit? Yes, you will because you know the outcome of breaking the speed limit.

When you know the outcome of disobeying Allah, in committing a sin, in breaking the commands of Allah, then you will not do so. When you know that sins lead to the path of Shaitan, and the path of Shaitan leads to the Fire, and that the Fire is an evil destination, then knowing the outcome of a sin and the consequences of it, deters you from committing that act. Sin is nothing but a moment of pleasure followed by a period of punishment.

Ibn Qayyim (رحمة الله عليه) has mentioned no less than 40 consequences of sins that a person will experience in this world alone. Some of these results are listed below:

1 – Being deprived of knowledge. For knowledge is light that Allah causes to reach the heart, and sin extinguishes that light. When Imam Shafi (رحمة الله عليه) sat before Imam Malik (رحمة الله عليه) and read to him, the latter admired the former because of the intelligence, alertness and understanding that he saw in him. He said, "I think that Allah has caused light to enter your heart, so do not extinguish it with the darkness of sin."

2 – Being deprived of provision. It is narrated that Thawbaan said:

42

"The Prophet ﷺ said: 'A man is deprived of provision because of the sins that he commits.'" (Ibn Majah).

3 – Sense of alienation that comes between a person and his Lord, and between him and other people. One of the righteous predecessors said: "If I disobey Allah, I see that in the attitude of my riding beast and my wife."

4 – Things become difficult for him, so that he does not turn his attention towards any matter but he finds the way blocked or he finds it difficult. By the same token, for the one who fears Allah, things are made easy.

5 – The sinner will find darkness in his heart, which he will feel just as he feels the darkness of night. So this darkness affects his heart as the physical darkness affects his vision. For obedience is light and disobedience is darkness.

> Abdullah ibn Abbas ﷺ said: "Good deeds make the face light, give light to the heart, and bring about ample provision, physical strength and love in people's hearts. Bad deeds make the face dark, give darkness to the heart, and bring about physical weakness, a lack of provision and hatred in people's hearts."

6 – Deprivation of worship and obedience. If sin brought no consequence other than that of preventing a person from doing an act of worship, that would be bad enough.

7 – Sin breeds sin until it dominates a person and he cannot escape from it.

8 – Sin weakens a person's willpower. It gradually strengthens his will to commit sins and weakens his will to repent until there is no will in his heart to repent at all. So he seeks forgiveness and expresses repentance, but they are merely words on the lips, like the repentance of the liars, whose hearts are still determined to commit sin and persist in it. This is one of the most serious consequences of sin.

9 – He will become desensitized and will no longer find sin abhorrent, so it will become his habit, and he will not be bothered if people see him commit a sin or talk about him.

> The Prophet (peace and blessings of Allah be upon him) said: "All of my nation (followers) will be fine except for those who sin openly, and that includes cases where Allah conceals a person's sins, but the following morning he exposes himself and says, 'O So and so, I did such and such last night, so he shamelessly exposes himself when all night his Lord had concealed his disobedience." (Bukhari and Muslim).

10 – When there are many sins they leave a mark on the heart of the person who commits them, so he becomes one of the negligent.

As one of the righteous predecessors said, concerning the verse:

$$كَلَّا ۖ بَلْ ۜ رَانَ عَلَىٰ قُلُوبِهِم مَّا كَانُوا يَكْسِبُونَ$$

> "Nay! But on their hearts is the Raan (covering of sins and evil deeds) which they used to earn" (Quran [3] 83:14) – interpretation of the meaning – this means sin upon sin. (Adda Wa Dawa, Ibn Qayyim)

Fourth Strategy – Insignificance and Worthlessness of Sins

The fourth strategy that will stop a person from committing a sin is to realise the insignificance of a sin. A person himself is doing right, but he compares himself to other people. He looks at those who are heedless, who don't care about the religion, who don't care about Allah and the Prophet ﷺ and he sees that these people seem to be doing sinning and enjoying life, whereas he doesn't have the pleasures and the luxuries that they have. If he feels that these sinners have a better life, or are in a better situation than he is, then he feels jealousy or envy. This is a big problem because focusing on sinners and the state that they are in invites a person to the path of sins.

I swear by Allah, if these sinners were to have just a moment of the peace that a righteous servant of Allah has, they would realize the insignificance and the worthlessness of the sins they commit.

A sinner enjoying all the pleasures of this world would be willing to sacrifice the entirety of his wealth for just one Sajdah, if only he realized the value of one Sajdah with Khushū'. This is not an exaggeration, because in the Hereafter we will truly realize the value of a righteous deed. There, we will realize the value of one Sajdah with sincerity, with Khushū', and we will say:

رَبِّ ارْجِعُونِ – لَعَلِّي أَعْمَلُ صَالِحًا فِيمَا تَرَكْتُ

"O my Lord! Send me back (to life), In order that I may work righteousness in the things I neglected." (Quran [1] 23:99-100)

If Allah makes your life difficult, tough and challenging, never assume it is because Allah loves the sinners. Never assume that Allah does not love you. Never think Allah has neglected you. When Allah does not abandon those who disobey Him, when Allah blesses the sinners with His blessings, then how can Allah neglect and hate those who obey Him? How can a person assume that after obeying Allah, after remembering Him day and night, that Allah does not love him or He has abandoned him?

A person who worships Allah, prays his Salah and obeys Him, such a person lives an unconstrained life. As long as he is on the straight path, no matter what problems and worries he may have in his life, his life is not bound. Your life is not hampered as long as you are in

Obstructions

the obedience of Allah. Life is constrained for a believer, if he misses his Fajr Salah. Life is constrained for him if he misses the first row in the Masjid. Life is constrained for him if he prays Salah without Khushū'. Life is constrained for him if he prostrates and Shaitan distracts him from his Lord. Your life is truly constrained for you, when something that brings you closer to Allah passes you by.

Never imagine that the life of heedlessness is a happy life, never imagine that a wealthy person's life is a happy life. If this were the case, then the happiest person would have been Qarun, who was living at the time of Musa ﷺ. The amount of wealth Allah gave him was such that he had to employ a group of strong men just to take care of the keys to his treasures. Yet he was of the worst of people mentioned in the Quran.

Fifth Strategy – spending free time in obedience to Allah

Do you think a person who spends his free time in the path of Allah, in doing righteous actions, will have time to even think about sins? Free time is a blessing from Allah, and many people use the phrase 'killing time' when wasting their free time, "I'm just killing some time." When a person is 'killing time', he is in one of two states. Either he is in a state of sinning or he is in a state of heedlessness: and both of these lead to the path of sins.

Never 'kill time', spend it instead in the path of Allah. Learn the Quran, study the meaning of it, study the commentaries on it, perform night prayers, perform voluntary fasts, listen to Islamic lectures, help people around you. When you spend your time in the path of Allah, you will never find time to disobey Him.

The question remains: How do I spend my free time in the path of Allah? What are the steps to take that will help me to be successful in spending my free time in Allah's obedience? The answer is to plan your day. As it is rightly said, when you fail to plan, you plan to fail. When you have a plan, this in and of itself shows your intention to spend your day in obedience to Allah.

How do I make a plan? When you wake up in the morning, the first thing that most people do is check their emails, they check their mobile phones to see if they've missed a call or a WhatsApp message; they check their Facebook accounts. Only then do they get ready to go to work. I am not saying that it is prohibited to start off your day in such a manner, but what I am saying is that when you begin your day with heedlessness and worldly matters, how can you expect your day to proceed in obedience to Allah? It's possible, but most unlikely!

The moment you open your eyes in the morning, start your day with the Du'as that the Prophet ﷺ taught us.

Morning and Evening Supplications from Authentic Hadiths

(1) The Prophet ﷺ said, "The most superior way of asking for forgiveness from Allah is:

اللَّهُمَّ أَنْتَ رَبِّي، لاَ إِلَهَ إِلاَّ أَنْتَ، خَلَقْتَنِي وَأَنَا عَبْدُكَ، وَأَنَا عَلَى عَهْدِكَ وَوَعْدِكَ مَا اسْتَطَعْتُ، أَعُوذُ بِكَ مِنْ شَرِّ مَا صَنَعْتُ، أَبُوءُ لَكَ بِنِعْمَتِكَ عَلَيَّ وَأَبُوءُ لَكَ بِذَنْبِي، فَاغْفِرْ لِي، فَإِنَّهُ لاَ يَغْفِرُ الذُّنُوبَ إِلاَّ أَنْتَ

O Allah, You are my Lord, there is none worthy of worship but You. You created me and I am your slave. I keep Your covenant, and my pledge to You so far as I am able. I seek refuge in You from the evil of what I have done. I admit to Your blessings upon me, and I admit to my misdeeds. Forgive me, for there is none who may forgive sins but You.

The Prophet ﷺ added, "If somebody recites it during the day with firm faith in it, and dies on the same day before the evening, he will be from [of] the people of

47

Paradise; and if somebody recites it at night with firm faith in it, and dies before the morning, he will be from [of] the people of Paradise." (Bukhari)

(2) A man came to the Prophet ﷺ and said: O Messenger of Allah, I was stung by a scorpion last night. He said:

"If you had said, when evening came:

أَعُوذُ بِكَلِمَاتِ اللهِ التَّامَّاتِ مِنْ شَرِّ مَا خَلَقَ ، لَمْ تَضُرَّكَ

I seek refuge in the perfect words of Allah from the evil of that which He has created."
It would not have harmed you. (Muslim)

(3) The Prophet ﷺ did not used to leave off these supplications whenever he entered the evening and whenever he entered the morning:

اللَّهُمَّ إِنِّي أَسْأَلُكَ الْعَافِيَةَ فِي الدُّنْيَا وَالْآخِرَةِ ، اللَّهُمَّ إِنِّي أَسْأَلُكَ الْعَفْوَ وَالْعَافِيَةَ فِي دِينِي وَدُنْيَايَ وَأَهْلِي وَمَالِي ، اللَّهُمَّ اسْتُرْ عَوْرَاتِي وَآمِنْ رَوْعَاتِي ، اللَّهُمَّ احْفَظْنِي مِنْ بَيْنِ يَدَيَّ ، وَمِنْ خَلْفِي ، وَعَنْ يَمِينِي ، وَعَنْ شِمَالِي ، وَمِنْ فَوْقِي ، وَأَعُوذُ بِعَظَمَتِكَ أَنْ أُغْتَالَ مِنْ تَحْتِي

O Allah, I ask you for well-being and security in this world and in the Hereafter. O Allah, I ask you for pardon and for security in my religion, my worldly life, my family and my wealth. O Allah, Conceal my faults and keep me safe from that which I fear. O Allah, guard me from in front of me and from behind me, and from my right and from my left, and from above me, and I seek refuge in Your greatness from being unexpectedly destroyed from beneath me. (Abu Dawood)

(4) When the Prophet ﷺ entered the evening he would say:

48

أَمْسَيْنَا وَأَمْسَى الْمُلْكُ لِلَّهِ ، وَالْحَمْدُ لِلَّهِ لَا إِلَهَ إِلَّا اللهُ ، وَحْدَهُ لَا شَرِيكَ لَهُ ، لَهُ الْمُلْكُ وَلَهُ الْحَمْدُ وَهُوَ عَلَى كُلِّ شَيْءٍ قَدِيرٌ ، رَبِّ أَسْأَلُكَ خَيْرَ مَا فِي هَذِهِ اللَّيْلَةِ وَخَيْرَ مَا بَعْدَهَا ، وَأَعُوذُ بِكَ مِنْ شَرِّ مَا فِي هَذِهِ اللَّيْلَةِ وَشَرِّ مَا بَعْدَهَا ، رَبِّ أَعُوذُ بِكَ مِنَ الْكَسَلِ وَسُوءِ الْكِبَرِ ، رَبِّ أَعُوذُ بِكَ مِنْ عَذَابٍ فِي النَّارِ وَعَذَابٍ فِي الْقَبْرِ وَإِذَا أَصْبَحَ قَالَ ذَلِكَ أَيْضًا : أَصْبَحْنَا وَأَصْبَحَ الْمُلْكُ لِلَّهِ

We have entered the evening, and sovereignty has entered the evening being for Allah alone, and all praise is for Allah. None has the right to be worshipped except Allah alone, having no partner. Sovereignty is for Him, and all praise is for Him, and He has full power over everything. O Allah, I ask you for the good that lies in this night and for the good of what comes after it, and I seek Your refuge from the evil that lies in this night and from the evil of what comes after it. O My Lord! I seek Your refuge from laziness and decrepit old age; and I seek Your refuge from punishment in the fire, and from punishment in the grave.

When he entered the morning he said: *We have entered the morning, and sovereignty has entered the morning being for Allah alone.* (and continued the supplication) (Muslim)

(5) Uthman Ibn Affan ؓ said:

I heard the Prophet ﷺ say, whoever says:

بِسْمِ اللهِ الَّذِي لَا يَضُرُّ مَعَ اسْمِهِ شَيْءٌ فِي الْأَرْضِ وَلَا فِي السَّمَاءِ وَهُوَ السَّمِيعُ الْعَلِيمُ

With the name of Allah, He whose name is such that when it is mentioned nothing in the earth or the heavens can cause harm, and He is the All-Hearing, the All-Knowing.

Whoever says it three times in the evening, will not be stuck by sudden calamity until morning; and whoever says it three times in the morning will not be struck by sudden calamity until the evening. (Abu Dawood)

First Step for your Daily Planner

When you wake up in the morning, ask yourself: What were the first words the Prophet ﷺ would utter in the morning?, Print these Du'as out and place them next to your bed, so that when you wake up in the morning, they are next to you and you don't forget to read them.

Start with any of the Du'as on day 1, and begin the next 3-5 days in the same way.

[There is no limit on the number of days to do this, but I am saying 3 days because the Prophet ﷺ said:

"The most beloved of deeds to Allah are the most consistent of them, even if they are few." (Bukhari and Muslim)]

The scholars say that when a person does a deed for 3 days it becomes a continuous act, which is what Allah likes. Therefore, if you make the habit of just one Dua, on the 3ʳᵈ continuous day, you will see the blessings of this in your life, in your wealth and you will see a positive change within yourself.

Once you make one good deed into a continuous act of yours, then move on to another deed, then the next. For example, read one page of the Quran every day, the translation of a page from the Quran, the commentary of a page from the Quran, or any other good deed, make it into a continuous act of yours.

When you have added these new good deeds to your daily plan, you will not have free time or 'time to kill', because the free time that you had is now being spent in obedience to Allah. As a result, by investing your free time in the path of Allah, will keep you away from sins.

Second Step for your Daily Planner

The second question to ask yourself for the benefit of your daily planner is: "What is one thing I can do that will make Allah pleased with me today?" This is the most important question to ask yourself day and night. Think about how you can please Allah. If you start your day with the intention of pleasing Allah, then with Allah's mercy you will not get caught up in sins.

On the other hand, if you wake up in the morning, and while you pray your Fajr Salah you are concerned about your wealth, your money, your car, what and where you will eat and drink today: when you make this world your primary concern, you are attaching your purpose in life to these worldly matters. Can you really then expect to be saved from sins and temptations? How is this possible?

I am by no means saying that you sit and wait for your provision to come to you: not at all. What I am saying is not to make your worldly life your primary or main concern. Rather, make your Hereafter your primary and main concern. The Prophet صلى الله عليه وسلم would make Du'a to Allah:

> "O Allah! Don't make the world our biggest concern"
> (Tirmidhi)

Let your greatest concern be that you may have performed your Sajdah absentmindedly during Salah.

Let your greatest concern be that you recited the Quran and your eyes never shed a tear.

Let your greatest concern be that you made Du'a to Allah and it may not have been accepted.

51

These are the things to be concerned about. Let your preoccupation with the Hereafter be your greatest concern: the same matter that the Prophets of Allah ﷺ were also most worried about. As a result they cried in their Salah, fearing Allah and the Hereafter.

Sixth Strategy – Visiting Graveyards

One of the strategies that will help a person stay away from sin is visiting graveyards frequently. Visiting graveyards reminds a person of the Hereafter; and by remembering the Hereafter, the world begins to appear insignificant, which weakens the influence of Shaitan. The Prophet ﷺ said:

كنت نهيتكم عن زيارة القبور ألا فزوروها فإنها تذكركم الآخرة

> I used to forbid you to visit graves, but now visit them, for they will remind you of the Hereafter. (Muslim)

Do not let a week pass by where you have not joined a funeral; because by attending a funeral, especially that of a close friend or a relative, it will increase the softening of your heart. When you reflect that this relative or friend was recently living amongst us, and today he is in his grave and no worldly thing is of any importance or benefit to him, such reflections will reduce this world to its true perspective in your eyes. They will remove temptation and keep you away from sins. On the other hand, these reflections will bring you closer to doing righteous deeds.

Seventh Strategy – Visiting the Sick

Visiting the sick is not only a duty owed by Muslims to one another, it also helps to keep us away from sins, because it makes us appreciate the blessings of Allah. When you reflect upon your own self and your well-being, and the good health that Allah has given you, it reminds you of your eyesight, your hearing and all the other healthy bodily organs you have been given: this introspection increases you in gratitude to Allah, which stops you from taking the path of sin.

Visit a sick person at least once a week, and remind yourselves of the blessings from Allah that you enjoy: this will distance you from disobedience to Allah.

Eighth Strategy – Repentance

Repentance is one of the most important strategies in helping you to stay away from sins. Many people think that repentance comes only after one has transgressed. Repentance is something to be done even without doing a sin. The Prophet ﷺ said:

والله إني لأستغفر الله وأتوب إليه في اليوم أكثر من سبعين مرة

I swear by Allah that I seek Allah's Pardon and turn to Him in repentance more than seventy times a day. (Bukhari)

The Prophet ﷺ had all his past and future sins forgiven by Allah *in advance*, yet he would repent to Allah many and many times a day. So, how much more do you think <u>we</u> should repent to Allah?

Don't wait to do a sin and then repent, repentance is not only for when you do a sin, repentance is required whether you do a sin or not:

طُوبَى لِمَنْ وَجَدَ فِي صَحِيفَتِهِ اسْتِغْفَارًا كَثِيرًا

He who wants his Register to please him should do a lot of Istighfar. (Ibn Majah)

Ninth Strategy – keeping away from Bad Company

The Prophet ﷺ said:

الْمَرْءُ عَلَى دِينِ خَلِيلِهِ فَلْيَنْظُرْ أَحَدُكُمْ مَنْ يُخَالِلْ

A man will follow the way of his close friends, so let each

one of you look at who he takes as a close friend. (Abu Dawood)

Do not keep bad company, because eventually they could lead you to the wrong path. Even if they don't influence you directly, it will make it difficult for you to stay on the right path when your friends are on the wrong path.

Suppose you are at college, and your college friends tell you to join them one day to go to the cinema. Since you are already part of their circle it will be difficult for you not to join them. This is how bad company and friends lead towards the wrong path.

Tenth Strategy – keeping away from places of temptation

The society that we are living in, i.e. western society, is filled with temptation – media of all types, magazines, flirting in the streets, satellite TV, the internet, etc... So you have to flee from all of these in order to keep your religious commitment sound.

What do you do when temptation comes your way?

We are human beings and therefore we will make mistakes and do wrong in our lives. Shaitan continues to whisper, and he will not leave you. He didn't leave Adam ﷺ. These ten strategies can help to keep you away from sins, yet temptations may come your way, so what should you do at that moment? The Prophet ﷺ said:

تُعْرَضُ الْفِتَنُ عَلَى الْقُلُوبِ كَالْحَصِيرِ عُودًا عُودًا فَأَيُّ قَلْبٍ أُشْرِبَهَا نُكِتَ فِيهِ نُكْتَةٌ سَوْدَاءُ وَأَيُّ قَلْبٍ أَنْكَرَهَا نُكِتَ فِيهِ نُكْتَةٌ بَيْضَاءُ حَتَّى تَصِيرَ عَلَى قَلْبَيْنِ عَلَى أَبْيَضَ مِثْلِ الصَّفَا فَلَا تَضُرُّهُ فِتْنَةٌ مَا دَامَتْ السَّمَاوَاتُ وَالْأَرْضُ وَالْآخَرُ أَسْوَدُ مُرْبَادًّا كَالْكُوزِ مُجَخِّيًا لَا يَعْرِفُ مَعْرُوفًا وَلَا يُنْكِرُ مُنْكَرًا

54

Temptations are offered to the hearts, just like the straws that are sewn into a woven mat, one after another. Any heart that accepts the temptation, then a black spot will be woven onto it. Any heart that rejects the temptation, then a white spot will be woven onto it. The hearts will therefore fall into two categories: white, just like a barren rock; no temptation shall ever harm this category as long as the heavens and earth still exist. The other category is black, just like a cup that is turned upside down, for this heart does not recognize righteousness or renounce evil. (Muslim)

The problem is not temptations coming and appearing on your heart, that's not a problem at all, as the Prophet ﷺ said, they are offered to the heart one after another, so no heart can escape temptations. The question is, what do you do with temptations once they come? Do you accept them or do you reject them? The way to reject temptation is by following the ten strategies we have listed. By rejecting temptation, white spots will be woven onto your heart, and as a result, no temptations shall ever harm this heart as long as the heavens and earth still exist.

Advice Regarding Sins

Never think of your past sins, never remind yourself of your failings except in a state of genuine remorse that might lead to a good deed and a sincere act of repentance. Shaitan reminds you of your sins so that you will eventually fall into his trap. For instance, Shaitan traps you by telling you that you are not a true believer: that although you repent to Allah, you turn to Allah, because you still commit sins, you are not truthful in your repentance, you are a hypocrite, and so on. This is how Shaitan traps a believer.

Therefore, only think of your past sins to take yourself towards sincere repentance. Never let your failings cause you to despair of the mercy of Allah, because desperation is from Shaitan. And when you despair of Allah, then this leads you into evil and bad thoughts about Allah.

This leads to statements such as, 'Allah will not forgive me', 'Allah will punish me', and so on. This is not befitting of a true believer. Keep good thoughts of Allah: say, 'O Allah, put my heart at peace and make my task easy for me', 'O Allah, keep me steadfast on my religion, O Allah, I repent to you, O Allah, I ask You for Your Mercy'. This will bring goodness and blessings from Allah.

The Prophet ﷺ said that Allah said:

أنا عند ظن عبدي بي إن ظن بي خيرا فله ، وإن ظن بي شرا فله

I am as my servant thinks of me. If he assumes good of Me then he will find good from his Lord. And if he assumes evil of me then he will find evil from his Lord. (Ahmed)

Keep good thoughts of Allah, and never make statements such as, 'Allah will not guide me', 'Allah will not forgive me', 'Allah will give me a bad ending'. Have good thoughts about Allah. Don't think evil of Allah. You are dealing with the King of all kings, the One Who is full of glory, and the One Who is the Most Gracious, the Most Merciful. Allah calls out to His servants and says:

يا عبادي ، لو أن أولكم وآخركم وإنسكم وجنكم كانوا على أتقى قلب رجل واحد منكم ما زاد ذلك في ملكي شيئا ، يا عبادي لو أن أولكم وآخركم وإنسكم وجنكم كانوا على أفجر قلب رجل واحد ما نقص ذلك من ملكي شيئا

O, My servants, if the first and the last of you and the human and the jinn of you were as pious as the most pious heart of anyone among you, it would not add anything to My dominion. O, My servants, if the first and the last of you and the human and the jinn of you were as wicked as the most wicked heart of anyone among you it would not decrease anything from My dominion. (Muslim)

How can you think badly of Allah, when He was the One who took you out from three layers of darkness? How can you think evil of Allah when He was the One Who guided you? How can you think evil of Allah when He was the One Who fed you every day? How can you have bad thoughts of Allah when He blesses with His provision to the ones who associate partners with Him: how much more will come to you, because you are praying to Him, making Du'a to Him, repenting to Him? So how can you have bad thoughts of Allah? Repent to Allah with sincere repentance and keep good thoughts of Him.

Obstructions

Consuming food that could harm others prevents Khushū'

The Prophet ﷺ prohibited eating certain food, which – due to their odour – could harm others. Onions and garlic have a very strong smell to them, so the Prophet ﷺ prohibited eating raw onion and garlic and coming to the Masjid. The Prophet ﷺ said:

من أكل البصل والثوم والكراث فلا يقربن مسجدنا الملائكة تتأذى
مما يتأذى منه بنو آدم

> He who has eaten onions or garlic or leeks should not approach our mosque, because the angels are also offended by the strong smells that offend the children of Adam. (Muslim)

So, foods that have a strong smell unless well cooked, like onions and garlic, can disturb the person praying next to you.

Imagine if you were in the Masjid and you are praying behind the Imam in congregation and the person standing next to you has just eaten raw onion before coming to the Masjid, and is standing next to you in the Salah, don't you think this would distract you from Khushū' in your Salah? For most, the odour would be a distraction to them. Therefore, besides being a distraction to others, odours can prevent them achieving Khushū' in Salah, and possibly you too.

The scholars have discouraged from attending Salah in the Masjid all those whose breath may be adversely affected by things that carry a bad smell, including smoking (shisha or tobacco), because this offends both the Muslims and the Angels. And it can distract many from Khushū' in their Salah.

The Importance and Virtues of Siwaak

In order to avoid causing bad smells that could disturb others, one

58

can follow the Sunnah of the Prophet ﷺ by doing Siwaak before coming for Salah. He ﷺ said:

السواك مطهرة للفم مرضاة للرب

Siwaak cleanses the mouth and pleases the Lord. (Nasai)

The Prophet ﷺ said:

لولا أن أشق على أمتي أو على الناس لأمرتهم بالسواك مع كل صلاة

If I had not found it hard for my followers or the people, I would have ordered them to clean their teeth with Siwaak for every prayer. (Bukhari)

The Prophet ﷺ said:

تُفَضَّلُ الصَّلاةُ الَّتِي يَسْتَاكُ لَهَا عَلَى الَّتِي لا يُسْتَاكُ لَهَا سَبْعِينَ ضِعْفًا

A Salah offered after one has used a Miswak [Siwaak] is 70 times superior to the Salah offered without it. (Bayhaqi)

He ﷺ further said:

إذا قام أحدكم يصلي من الليل فليستك، فإن أحدكم إذا قرأ في صلاته وضع ملك فاه على فيه، ولا يخرج من فيه شيء إلا دخل فم الملك

Whenever one of you wakes up at night, he should use the Siwaak, because whenever any of you recites during his prayer, an angel places his mouth on the mouth of the one who recites and whenever any verse is recited, it goes directly into the mouth of this angel. (Sahih Al-Jame)

This shows the importance of cleansing our mouths before going for Salah, so that if there is any unpleasant smell, it does not harm

Obstructions

the angels nor the believers. Furthermore, removing any unpleasant smell will help in developing Khushū' in your Salah and the Salah of other believers who are in the Masjid.

Contrary to this, when there is an unpleasant smell, then not only does it harm the angels and the believers, it also prevents Khushū' in your own and in the Salah of those close to you. The minds would be distracted due to the unpleasant smell rather than concentrating on the recitation of the Quran and on the Salah.

Avoid praying in places where there are distractions

Photos, pictures and images hanging on the wall are very common distractions in Salah. Imagine that you are praying Salah and in front of you there is a picture or a photo of someone hanging on the wall. Wouldn't it distract you or at least decrease the level of Khushū' in your Salah?

The scholars are unanimously agreed that it is not allowed to pray in a place in which there are images of animate beings.

> Al-Nawawi said: "As for fabric on which there are images or crossed lines or anything that distracts the worshipper, it is makrūh to pray in it, facing towards it, or on it." (Al Majmoo)

This is because the Prophet ﷺ said:

لا تدخل الملائكة بيتًا فيه كلب ولا صورة

> Angels do not enter a house in which there is a dog or a picture. (Bukhari and Muslim)

The angels bring mercy and their presence is mercy. By having images and pictures of animated beings on our walls at home and around our houses we ourselves have closed the doors of mercy. When the angels do not enter a house in which there is a picture then how can we expect mercy from Allah? And how can we expect our Salah and Du'as to be accepted?

Aisha ؓ had a patterned curtain with which she covered the side of her house. The Prophet ﷺ said:

أميطي عني فإنه لا تزال تصاويره تعرض لي في صلاتي

> "Take this patterned curtain of yours away from us

Obstructions

61

because its images kept distracting me in my prayer."
(Bukhari)

If there are any distractions that would cause the level of your Khushū' to diminish, then avoid praying in that room, or remove those images: even if they are non-animated images, remove them.

Some prayer mats have permissible non-animated images and designs and they can cause so much distraction in a person's Salah, that instead of concentrating in the Salah, the mind keeps wondering towards the designs and the patterns on the prayer mat. Avoid such prayer mats, and buy simple ones without any designs and patterns on them.

Interlacing Fingers

Interlacing ones fingers and cracking them is a permissible act, however it is makruh. Whether a person does this in his Salah or even if he is on his way to perform Salah, in either case it is an act that is disliked. The reason why it is disliked for the one going to the Masjid for Salah is because the one who is headed towards the Masjid comes under the same ruling as one who is praying Salah. The Prophet ﷺ said:

إِذَا تَوَضَّأَ أَحَدُكُمْ فَأَحْسَنَ وُضُوءَهُ ثُمَّ خَرَجَ عَامِدًا إِلَى الْمَسْجِدِ فَلاَ يُشَبِّكَنَّ يَدَيْهِ فَإِنَّهُ فِي صَلاَةٍ

If any of you performs ablution, and performs his ablution perfectly, and then goes out intending for the mosque, he should not cross the fingers of his hand because he is already in prayer. (Abu Dawood)

The prohibition applies only to the one who is praying and the one who is heading towards the masjid, because it is a kind of fidgeting and not focusing with proper humility. (Ibn Hajar, Fathul Bari, 1 / 565)

Some worshippers during Salah fidget with their fingers by cracking them. This cracking of fingers does not befit one who is standing before Allah. This is also a sign of lack of Khushū', because if the heart is focused then the limbs would also be focused and be still.

Imagine being in the presence of the king, and cracking your fingers whilst you were standing in front of him, would you do this? I am sure you wouldn't. Therefore, if you wouldn't do this before a king, then how about doing so before the King of all kings? How about in front of the one who is constantly showering blessings upon you every moment of your life?

Interlacing the fingers is, therefore, disliked for the one who is going to Salah, waiting for the Salah, or during Salah. Outside of the state of Salah interlacing fingers is permissible.

Obstructions

Yawning during Salah

The act of yawning is disliked by Allah, and whatever Allah dislikes we should also dislike. The Prophet ﷺ said:

إن الله يحب العطاس ويكره التثاؤب، والتثاؤب من الشيطان فإذا تثاءب أحدكم فليرده ما استطاع فإن أحدكم إذا تثاءب فقال : هاها يضحك منه الشيطان

> Allah loves the sneeze and dislikes the yawn. As for yawning it is from Shaitan, if any one of you feels the urge to yawn, let him resist it as much as he can, and do not say 'Hah, hah' (do not make a noise when yawning), for it amuses Shaitan. (Bukhari)

Yawning is a sign of lethargy, and it is not possible for a person who has Khushū' to yawn during his Salah. Yawning makes Shaitan happy and he laughs. Therefore, following the tips and techniques that I am sharing with you here will help you to reduce yawning in your Salah. If a person does feel the urge to yawn in his Salah, then he should try to stifle it. The Prophet ﷺ said:

إِذَا تَثَاءَبَ أَحَدُكُمْ فَلْيَضَعْ يَدَهُ عَلَى فِيهِ وَإِذَا قَالَ آهْ آهْ فَإِنَّ الشَّيْطَانَ يَضْحَكُ مِنْ جَوْفِهِ

> If any of you yawns, let him place his hand over his mouth. If he says 'Hah, hah!' (makes a noise when yawning), Shaitan laughs from within him. (Tirmidhi)

The Prophet ﷺ taught us to resist yawning, if you fail to do so, then cover your mouth with your hands. When yawning, he ﷺ taught us to suppress any sound or noise.

It is simply unimaginable for a person with Khushū' to stand knowingly and consciously before Allah, before his Lord, before the

Creator of the heavens and the earth, before the Master of the Day of Judgement and openly yawn in that position. This is not consistent with Khushū' and that is why the Prophet ﷺ never yawned in his Salah.

ما تثاءب النبي صلى الله عليه وسلم في صلاة قط

> The Prophet ﷺ never yawned in His Salah. (Ibn Abi Shaybah, Bukhari in his Tareekh)

The Prophet ﷺ had the most Khushū' in his Salah, and because yawning is a sign of laziness, it pleases Shaitan; the Prophet ﷺ never yawned in his Salah because it leads to sluggishness in Salah instead of Khushū'.

Fiddling around during Salah

The Prophet ﷺ said:

أُمِرْتُ أَنْ أَسْجُدَ عَلَى سَبْعَةِ أَعْظُمٍ ، وَلَا أَكُفَّ ثَوْبًا وَلَا شَعْرًا

"I have been ordered to prostrate on seven bones and not to gather the clothes or the hair."

عن أبي رافع قال مر بي النبي صلى الله عليه وسلم وأنا ساجد قد عقصت شعري فحله أو قال فنهاني عنه

Abu Rafi ؓ narrates, the Prophet ﷺ passed by me whilst I was in prostration, my hair was braided. So He untied it or he said He forbade me from doing this.

Al-Nawawi (رحمة الله عليه) said:

The scholars are unanimously agreed that it is not permissible to pray with one's sleeves or garment rolled up and the like, or with one's hair braided or with one's hair wrapped up beneath the turban and so on. None of these things is permissible according to the consensus of the scholars, and it is makrūh in the sense of being discouraged and not proper. If a person prays like that, it is wrong to do so, nevertheless, his prayer remains valid. (Commentary of Muslim, 209)

Nowadays, some worshippers fiddle with their clothes, their hair, their beards during their Salah, without realizing that this is the place for Khushū'. When a person stands in his Salah, and fiddles with his hair, clothes, glasses, beard or watch, how can he develop Khushū'?

Imagine a person, having an audience with the king, a royal king of this world. Would he fiddle around with his clothes? If not, then why do so when standing before the King of all kings? Why do so when standing before the Lord of the heavens and the earth?

Therefore, when standing in Salah, unroll your sleeves, as it is easy to forget to unroll the sleeves after ablution. Do not fiddle with any part of your body, with your hair, clothes, beard, etc. Take full advantage of this short time of standing in Salah, and pray this Salah as though it were your last: the last time in your life that you are standing before Allah.

إذا قمت في صلاتك فصلِّ صلاة مودع

> When you stand up to pray, perform your prayer as if it were your last (Ibn Majah)

This moment of standing in Salah is your time for speaking with Allah, with your Lord, Your Creator, the One who provides for you, the One who cares for you more than anyone in this world, the One who loves you more than your mother, the One who gave you the ability to stand in front of him. Speak with Him and ask your needs from Him, standing in front of Him, sitting at His door step, prostrating to Allah: this is what is meant by this statement of the Prophet ﷺ:

أن تعبد الله كأنك تراه ، فإن لم تكن تراه ، فإنه يراك

> You worship Allah as though you can see Him. And if you cannot see Him, then (do know that) He sees you. (Bukhari and Muslim)

Obstructions

Wiping the forehead during Salah

The Prophet ﷺ would not wipe the traces of mud from his forehead.

عَنْ أَبِي سَلَمَةَ، قَالَ سَأَلْتُ أَبَا سَعِيدٍ قَالَ رَأَيْتُ رَسُولَ اللَّهِ صلى الله عليه وسلم يَسْجُدُ فِي الْمَاءِ وَالطِّينِ، حَتَّى رَأَيْتُ أَثَرَ الطِّينِ فِي جَبْهَتِهِ

Abu Saeed saw the Prophet ﷺ prostrating in mud and water and he saw the traces of mud on his forehead. (Bukhari)

This act of wiping off dust is disliked during Salah, however after Salah it is permissible. The reason why the Prophet ﷺ would not wipe away the traces of mud during Salah is because it would decrease the level of Khushū' in Salah.

The focus and concentration must be as much as we can manage during Salah, and being engaged in wiping the forehead or any other part of the body distracts you from developing Khushū' in your Salah.

Straightening the prayer mat during Salah

The Prophet ﷺ said:

إِذَا قَامَ أَحَدُكُمْ إِلَى الصَّلَاةِ فَإِنَّ الرَّحْمَةَ تُوَاجِهُهُ فَلَا يَمْسَحُ الْحَصَى

"When one of you stands for the Salah, mercy is facing him. Therefore, he should not wipe away the pebbles."
(Abu Dawood)

The Prophet ﷺ talked about a man levelling the earth on prostrating, and said:

" إِنْ كُنْتَ فَاعِلاً فَوَاحِدَةً "

"If you have to do so, then do it once." (Bukhari)

During Salah, it is not appropriate to level the earth, prayer mat or wipe away the pebbles, and the scholars consider it to be makruh. The reason is simply because you are standing in front of Allah, He is looking at you and hearing you perform Salah in a manner that befits His Majesty. So if at that moment you start to level the earth or straighten the prayer mat repeatedly, then you are spending that quality time behind your prayer mat instead of spending it before Allah.

The prayer mat or the place where you are praying should be prepared before you begin your Salah, so the need to straighten it does not arise during the prayer. If the need does arise, then do not do it more than once, because doing it repeatedly will distract your mind and concentration in Salah and as a result the level of Khushū' in your Salah will decrease, which is not what you want.

Obstructions

Resisting the need to relieve oneself

Try to imagine praying Salah and needing to urinate or pass wind, and trying to withold the urge in order not to break your ablution, do you think your mind will be focused on Salah? Most certainly, your mind, throughout the Salah, will be focused on holding onto your ablution. So because such a condition decreases the level of Khushū' and distracts a persons mind during Salah, the Prophet ﷺ said:

لا يأتي أحدكم الصلاة وهو حاقن حتى يتخفف

"None of you should come to prayer while one is feeling the call of nature until one eases oneself." (Abu Dawood)

Aisha ؓ narrates, she heard the Prophet ﷺ say:

لاَ يُصَلَّى بِحَضْرَةِ الطَّعَامِ وَلاَ وَهُوَ يُدَافِعُهُ الأَخْبَثَانِ

"Prayer should not be offered in the presence of meals, nor at the moment when one is struggling with the two evils (i.e. when one is feeling the call of nature)" (Abu Dawood)

Therefore, with regard to holding onto urination or passing of wind, because it would distract a person's mind whilst praying Salah, the Prophet ﷺ advised us to ease ourselves beforehand.

Whispers of Shaitan and Its Cure

One of the main obstructions to Khushū' in Salah and what most people complain about is the whispering of Shaitan. Many people complain that the whispers of Shaitan are the cause of distraction and lack of Khushū' in their Salah. First, since Salah is one of the greatest acts of worship, Shaitan will come and distract you at that moment because you are engaged in the greatest act of worship.

One time a Companion, Uthman ibn Abil A'as ﷺ, came to the Prophet ﷺ complaining about whispers in his Salah: He said "O Prophet of Allah, the Shaitan comes between me and my prayers and my recitation, confusing me therein." The Messenger of Allah ﷺ said:

ذاك شيطان يقال له خنزب فإذا أحسسته فتعوذ بالله منه واتفل على يسارك ثلاثا قال ففعلت ذلك فأذهبه الله عني

"That is a devil called Khanzab. If he affects you seek refuge in Allah from him and spit drily to your left three times." He [the Companion] said, "I did that and Allah took him away from me." (Muslim)

This Hadith shows that there is a specific Shaitan (whose name is Khanzab) appointed to distract those who are in their Salah from concentrating and focusing. This also shows that Shaitan is trying his best to distract you from developing Khushū'. He does not want you to focus in your Salah, and distracts you through his whispers every time you begin Salah. So you may find you have finished praying Salah and he has succeeded in distracting you throughout. This could mean that (if you do not do anything about it and you don't cure this problem through the remedies I am going to share with you here,) he will continue to distract you in your Salah every time you stand in prayer. Which means that you might never pray a Salah without any distractions.

Obstructions

There is no greater loss than that of leaving this world without performing a Sajdah with Khushū'. The time will come very soon when we will realize the value of just one Sajdah with Khushū' and sincerity; that time is when we leave this world for the Hereafter. There we will realize the true value of every Sajdah with Khushū'.

The scholars (amongst the righteous predecessors) said that a person might have prayed Salah for 40 years without one Salah being recorded for him. So this is a serious problem, and if you don't do anything about this, then you could be praying for many years with not one of those Salah being recorded in your favour.

Shaitan's whisper is a sign of Faith

The fact that Shaitan whispers to you is a sign of faith. Some people end up losing hope, they think they are lost or irretrievably doomed. One must never think in this way. The very fact that Shaitan is whispering to you is *because* you have sincerity and iman. Had you never had iman he would not have tried so hard to distract you with his whispers.

Some of the Companions complained to the Prophet ﷺ about the whispers that were bothering them. They came to the Prophet ﷺ and said to him:

"We find in ourselves thoughts that are too terrible to speak of." He said, "Are you really having such thoughts?" They said, "Yes." He said, "That is a clear sign of faith.'" (Muslim).

"The Prophet's words, 'That is a clear sign of faith' means that the very fact that you think of these whispers as something terrible, and that you are concerned about them, is a clear sign of faith. It is the sign of one who has achieved perfect faith." (Commentary of Muslim, Imam Nawawi)

Every time a person wants to turn to Allah, Shaitan wants to block the way, therefore, never think that just because Shaitan whispers, that you are lost or doomed. That's why [when] it was said to one of the Salaf that the Jews and Christians say, "We do not experience whispers," he said, "They are speaking the truth, for what would the Shaitan do with a house in ruins?" (Fatawa Ibn Taymiyyah)

Shaitans are of the Jinn and Mankind

Before moving onto the remedies for dealing with the whispering of Shaitan, we should realize that Shaitans are of two types. One is of the jinns and the other is of the human kind, and Allah reminds us in the last Surah of the Quran to seek protection from the whispers of the jinns and mankind. Allah says:

$$الَّذِي يُوَسْوِسُ فِي صُدُورِ النَّاسِ مِنَ الْجِنَّةِ وَالنَّاسِ$$

who whispers into the hearts of Mankind— Among Jinns and among Men. (Quran [1] 114 5-6)

Try to imagine: one day before you start to pray Salah, your friend who is waiting to go out with you after Salah, tells you, "Pray Salah quickly so that we can go out". If you accept this suggestion from your friend, would this increase or decrease the Khushū' in your Salah? Most probably it will decrease your Khushū'.

These are the Shaitans from mankind, who are whispering to you, and as a result these Shaitans are preventing you from developing Khushū' in your Salah. The cure for the whispers of Shaitan that I am going to share with you is to be used for both Shaitans of the jinns and mankind.

First Cure – Du'a

There is no greater cure for the whispers of Shaitan than making Du'a to Allah. Ask Allah to help you, make Du'a to Him and say, 'O Allah, I am weak, O Allah I need your help, O Allah help me and

73

seek refuge in Allah from Shaitan the outcast, saying:

أعوذ بالله من الشيطان الرجيم

I seek refuge in Allah from Shaitan the outcast.

As it was written in the Hadith mentioned above of Uthman ibn Abil A'as ﷺ.

Further, Allah says in the Quran:

وَإِمَّا يَنْزَغَنَّكَ مِنَ الشَّيْطَانِ نَزْغٌ فَاسْتَعِذْ بِاللَّهِ

And should a stroke from Shaitan (Satan) strike you, seek refuge with Allah. (Quran [2] 41:36)

Since you are seeking refuge in the Greatest, that is Allah, then Allah will help you, because He is the Greatest. And if Allah helps you, then none can overcome you. Allah says:

إِنْ يَنْصُرْكُمُ اللَّهُ فَلَا غَالِبَ لَكُمْ وَإِنْ يَخْذُلْكُمْ فَمَنْ ذَا الَّذِي يَنْصُرُكُمْ مِنْ بَعْدِهِ وَعَلَى اللَّهِ فَلْيَتَوَكَّلِ الْمُؤْمِنُونَ

If Allah helps you, none can overcome you: if He forsakes you, who is there after that that can help you? In Allah, then, let believers put their trust. (Quran: [1] 3:160)

So make Du'a to Allah in abundance especially in times when Du'as are accepted, like during the last portion of the night and on Fridays and so on.

Besides making Du'a to Allah, make the removal of the whispers your greatest concern. Because when Allah plans goodness for a servant of His, He makes the Hereafter the greatest concern for him. So when the matters of the Hereafter become your greatest concern, then you will make Du'a for it in abundance.

What is your Greatest Concern?

Let me ask you some simple questions: your answers will tell you what your greatest concern is. What is it that would make you most happy? What is it that would make you cry the most? What is it that worries you the most? What is the first thing that you think of when you wake up in the morning? What is the last thing in your mind before you sleep at night? Whatever your answers to these questions are will reveal your greatest concern. If the answer to these questions is something related to the Hereafter, if it has to do with things that will bring you closer to Allah, then alhumdulillah. If not, then *from now on*, make things that relate to the Hereafter your greatest concern. The Prophet ﷺ would make this Du'a to Allah:

اللهم لا تجعل الدنيا اكبر همنا

O Allah, don't make this world our biggest concern. (Tirmidhi)

There is nothing more worth worrying about than those things that are obstructing you or stopping you from getting closer to Allah. Everything in this world is insignificant compared to Allah and those actions that bring a servant closer to Allah.

Therefore, make any obstacles that are coming between you and Allah your greatest concern. When you make them your greatest concern, then you will increase in your Du'a to Allah.

Second Cure – constantly rejecting Shaitan's whispers

Shaitan only has one power, that of whispering to you. Shaitan does not have the power to make you do what he wants. Allah has given every one of us free will. So if this is the only ability of Shaitan, then when he does whisper, the question is what do you do about that whisper? Do you accept it or do you reject it?

If you accept his whisper and you go along with his distractions, then he will continue whispering to you and that will result in your having to suffer more and more whispers. On the other hand, if you reject it by refocusing on your Salah, by refocusing on your recitation and by refocusing on your awareness of standing before Allah, then you will have rejected his whispers and achieving this will help your development of Khushū' in Salah.

Therefore, as long as you keep on bringing your focus back to your recitation in Salah and to your awareness of standing before Allah, then you are on the way to developing Khushū'. The Prophet ﷺ said:

تُعْرَضُ الْفِتَنُ عَلَى الْقُلُوبِ كَالْحَصِيرِ عُودًا عُودًا فَأَيُّ قَلْبٍ أُشْرِبَهَا نُكِتَ فِيهِ نُكْتَةٌ سَوْدَاءُ وَأَيُّ قَلْبٍ أَنْكَرَهَا نُكِتَ فِيهِ نُكْتَةٌ بَيْضَاءُ حَتَّى تَصِيرَ عَلَى قَلْبَيْنِ عَلَى أَبْيَضَ مِثْلِ الصَّفَا فَلَا تَضُرُّهُ فِتْنَةٌ مَا دَامَتْ السَّمَاوَاتُ وَالْأَرْضُ وَالْآخَرُ أَسْوَدُ مُرْبَادًا كَالْكُوزِ مُجَخِّيًا لَا يَعْرِفُ مَعْرُوفًا وَلَا يُنْكِرُ مُنْكَرًا

Temptations are offered to the hearts, just like the straws that are sewn into a woven mat, one after another. Any heart that accepts the temptation, then a black dot will be woven onto it. Any heart that rejects the temptation, then a white dot will be woven onto it. The hearts will therefore fall into two categories: white, just like a barren rock; no temptation shall ever harm this category as long as the heavens and earth still exist. The other category is black, just like a cup that is turned upside down, for this heart does not recognize righteousness or renounce evil. (Muslim)

The thoughts that come into your mind are very important because your thoughts determine your destiny. Here is what is said about thoughts:

"Mind your thoughts for they become your words;

Mind your words for they become your actions;
Mind your actions for they become your habits;
Mind your habits for they become your character;
Mind your character for it becomes your destiny."
(Charles Reade)

So you need to monitor your thoughts, because they determine your destiny. However, since we don't have any control over our thoughts, and none of us can escape the thoughts that come into our minds, what *can* we do?

While we do not have control over what kind of thoughts come into our mind, we definitely have control over what kinds of thoughts we choose to dwell on.

So the question is what do you do with those thoughts? Do you accept them or do you reject them?

Try to imagine that Shaitan insinuates an evil thought about a person into your mind. Shaitan whispers to you that person x thinks badly of you without good cause. This evil suspicion from Shaitan is out of your control, but you have two choices. You may accept it, believe in it and start to tell others that person x thinks badly of you, which means you have accepted Shaitan's whisper. Or, the second choice is that the moment Shaitan whispered into your heart about person x, though his whispers are not under your control, you can choose not to let it reach your tongue: reject the idea and purify your heart from any kind of evil thought about the person in question. That is the way you can reject the whispers of Shaitan.

The problem is not Shaitan's whispering to you, because that is beyond your control. What is within your control is the will to reject his whispers, and once you systematically reject his whispers by refocusing on your Salah, - if Allah wills - this will help you to increase your level of Khushū'.

Obstructions

If Shaitan whispers 10 times in one rak'ah, make sure you bring yourself back to the Salah. Every time you receive his whisper, just remember, return to your Salah, return to your Khushū', refocus on your recitation, and as long as you bring yourself back all is well. Eventually, with perseverance, your heart and mind will become trained in rejecting these whispers.

Many of my students have followed this advice; they have tried and tested this method and, with the grace of Allah, almost all of them benefitted from this method and trained their hearts well to reject the whispers of Shaitan.

This rejection of the whispers of Shaitan will increase the Khushū' in your Salah. As long as you are developing and increasing your Khushū', and each Salah continues to improve upon the previous one, then you are on the right path for developing the habit of Khushū'.

Third Cure –engaging in acts of worship outside of Salah

Imagine a person who has made this world his greatest concern: he is mainly bothered about earning money, owning flashy cars, and so forth. His whole life revolves around the pleasures of this world. If such a person whose life is full of heedlessness comes and stands in Salah, how can his lifestyle help him towards developing Khushū' in his Salah? How can he expect to have Khushū' in his Salah, when his entire life revolves around the pleasures of this world? It is not possible.

Outside of your Salah, you need to engage yourself in other acts of worship, especially in these times, when there are so many different temptations out there distracting us: the TV, Magazines, the Internet, and many many others. If you don't stay engaged in acts of worship outside of Salah, then how can you expect to stand in Salah and maintain concentration and focus?

Holding onto the Quran

There is nothing that better eliminates the whispers of Shaitan, and brings a person closer to Allah, than the Quran. The happiest person in the world is the one who loves to recite the Quran, the one who loves to listen to the Quran, the one who loves to understand and ponder over the Quran, the one who loves to act upon the Quran.

There are two important points here with regards to the recitation of the Quran.

The first point related to Quran is to read the Quran together with the translation if you do not understand the Arabic. Yes, you will still get the reward for reading the Arabic portion alone, but if you do not understand Arabic, and you don't know what Allah's message to you is, then how is this going to soften your heart, and how are you going to benefit from the message of the Quran? The main reason for the Quran's revelation is its guidance for mankind. Allah says in the Quran:

شَهْرُ رَمَضَانَ الَّذِي أُنْزِلَ فِيهِ الْقُرْآنُ هُدًى لِلنَّاسِ وَبَيِّنَاتٍ مِنَ الْهُدَى وَالْفُرْقَانِ

Ramadan is the (month) in which was sent down the Quran as a guide to mankind also clear (Signs) for guidance and judgment (between right and wrong). (Quran [1] 2:185)

Therefore, when you read the Quran, divide your time into half. Half of the time read the Arabic portion and the other half of the time read the translation of it in the language you understand the best. This way, you will get more reward for reading the Quran, and when you follow its guidance through understanding it, then you will get extra rewards for following it.

The second point related to the Quran is that many people

complain that they don't have time to read the Quran. Some complain that when they sit with the Quran they become lethargic, and they end up not reciting but closing it. The counteractions to this situation are three:

The first cure is turning to Allah with sincere repentance. This is because sins act as a barrier between a person and the mercy of Allah. That is why Allah says in the Quran:

$$\text{لَوْلَا تَسْتَغْفِرُونَ اللَّهَ لَعَلَّكُمْ تُرْحَمُونَ}$$

Why do you not seek forgiveness from Allah, so that you are treated with mercy? (Qur'an [2] 27:46b-c)

The second cure is realizing the greatness of the Quran. The fact that a person feels lethargic when starting to recite the Quran is because until now he has not realized its greatness. When you realize that the Quran is the Book from Allah, and had it was sent down on a mountain, they would have fallen down in utter ruin.

"In the Quran there is news of what happened before you, and information about what is to come after you, and judgement concerning what is happening among you. It is the Criterion without jest. It is the firm rope of Allah, it is the Wise Reminder, and it is the Straight Path. It is the Book that whims and desires cannot distort and tongues cannot twist. Scholars have never tired of it. It never becomes dull from continual recitation, and its wonders never end. It is the one that when the jinns heard it, they did not hesitate to say about it, "Verily! We have heard a wonderful Recital (this Quran)! It guides to the Right Path." [Al-Jinn: 1-2] "Whoever speaks according to it has uttered the truth; whoever acts according to it is rewarded; whoever judges by it has judged justly; and whoever calls to it [is] guided to the straight path." (Tirmidhi)

When you realize that this is the book you are holding in your hand, then how can one feel lethargic towards it?

The third cure is to make a firm resolution to recite a portion of the Quran daily and on a consistent basis. The way to do this is to set yourself a portion that you can commit to on a daily basis. Don't make your daily amount so big that you won't be able to keep it up over a sustained period. The Prophet ﷺ said:

$$أحب الأعمال إلى الله تعالى أدومها وإن قل$$

The deeds most loved by Allah (are those) done regularly, even if they are small. (Muslim)

So set yourself a portion that you can easily maintain with consistency. In this way it is much easier than you imagine, and will become a regular habit after three days of practice.

When an average person dedicates eight hours a day to work in order to feed himself and his family, then what about the food and the nourishment for your soul? The food for your soul is the Quran. So when an average person spends eight hours a day to feed his body, then how can he not devote 20 minutes a day to feed his soul?

It is really easy, and not difficult at all, the question simply remains: are you going to do it or not? Are you a person of action or not? Make your decision RIGHT NOW, and ACT ON IT TODAY!

Holding onto the daily authentic Du'as

Amongst the acts of worship to be engaged in outside Salah are the authentic Du'as of the Prophet ﷺ from the Hadith. These Du'as remind you of Allah constantly at all times; when you eat, when you drink, when you wake up in the morning, when you do anything. As long as you recite these Du'as with understanding and with firm belief in Allah, and then you stand in Salah, it will reduce the whispers of Shaitan. On the other hand, you cannot ignore

Obstructions

Allah throughout the day, in heedlessness giving your attention to all the temptations around you; the TV, Magazines, Internet, Facebook, WhatsApp...and then when you stand up for Salah, you complain of the whispers of Shaitan. Of course Shaitan will whisper, because throughout the day you paid no attention to Allah, you ignored Him throughout the day, you were totally heedless of Him, and then you expect to stand up in Salah and be free of the whispers of Shaitan?

In order for this step to work, make sure that you understand what you are asking from Allah in your Du'as. If you don't understand Arabic, then when reciting the Du'as in Arabic, make sure that you know the translation of the Du'as you are making to Allah. Because the number one thing that guarantees the acceptance of your Du'a is sincerity, and how can a person who does not understand what he is asking Allah for be sincere in his Du'as?

When you are sincere in your daily Du'as, and then you stand for Salah, then there is less chance of Shaitan distracting you, because you were already engaged in the remembrance of Allah throughout the day. Therefore, these daily Du'as help in eliminating the whispers of Shaitan.

Dhikr (remembrance of Allah)

Allah says in the Quran:

$$\text{أَلَا بِذِكْرِ اللَّهِ تَطْمَئِنُّ الْقُلُوبُ}$$

Verily, in the remembrance of Allah do hearts find rest. (Quran [3] 13:28)

$$\text{وَلَذِكْرُ اللَّهِ أَكْبَرُ}$$

Remembrance of Allah indeed is the greatest (thing in life) [virtue]. (Quran [1] 29:45)

Throughout the day, whilst you are sitting, walking, driving your car, constantly engage yourself in glorifying Him, praising Him and extolling His greatness.

$$ يَا أَيُّهَا الَّذِينَ آمَنُوا اذْكُرُوا اللَّهَ ذِكْرًا كَثِيرًا – وَسَبِّحُوهُ بُكْرَةً وَأَصِيلًا $$

O you who believe! Remember Allah with much remembrance. And glorify His Praises morning and afternoon. (Quran [3] 33:41-2)

A person may ask, "How can I do dhikr of Allah throughout the day, when I'm at work, and so on?"

There are two types of Dhikr: Dhikr with the tongue such as reciting the Quran, Du'as, tasbih (saying Subhan Allah), takbir (saying Allahu Akbar) etc; and Dhikr in the heart, which means thinking of Allah and His greatness and power, or reciting the Quran in one's heart. This does not bring the same reward as reading the Quran, because the reward has to do with reading, which can only be done on the tongue (by moving the tongue and speaking the words).

The proof that this distinction is made between the two kinds of Dhikr is the fact that the scholars are agreed that it is permissible for a person who is junub (in a state of impurity following sexual activity) to recite the Quran in his heart, but it is prohibited for him to recite it out loud or utter it.

> Al-Nawawi said: (The scholars) are agreed that if a person who is junub thinks of [the] Quran in his heart, without moving his tongue, he is not reciting it in the way that is forbidden for one who is junub. (Commentary of Muslim, Nawawi 4/103)

Therefore, if you are unable to make Dhikr of Allah with your tongue then make Dhikr of Him in your heart. If you remember Allah throughout the day, then you will also remember Him in your Salah. On the other hand, if you don't make the effort to remember Allah throughout the day and you only think of yourself

Obstructions

and your work, what you are going to get up to today, what you are going to eat and drink today and the pleasures of this world, then how can you remember Allah in your Salah? It's possible, but very unlikely.

That's why when a man complained to the Prophet ﷺ, "The laws of Islam are too heavy for me, so tell me something that I can easily follow," the Prophet ﷺ told him:

لا يزال لسانك رطبا من ذكر الله عز وجل

"Let your tongue be always busy with the remembrance of Allah." (Ahmad).

Voluntary Fasting

Fasting is a type of worship that brings a person closer to Allah. It is the best method of training yourself for doing good deeds. Because it is not just abstention from eating and drinking that is required when you fast. The main purpose of fasting is to develop God consciousness and righteousness. Allah says in the Quran:

يَا أَيُّهَا الَّذِينَ آمَنُوا كُتِبَ عَلَيْكُمُ الصِّيَامُ كَمَا كُتِبَ عَلَى الَّذِينَ مِنْ قَبْلِكُمْ لَعَلَّكُمْ تَتَّقُونَ

O you who believe, the fasts have been enjoined upon you as they were enjoined upon those before you, so that you may be God-fearing. (Quran [2] 2:183)

Therefore, when you fast, besides abstaining from eating and drinking, your tongue is also fasting, your ears are fasting, and your eyes are fasting. Which means that you do not speak evil, you do not listen to evil, you do not look at (or for) evil, and you do not think evil. Fasting is an act of self-restraint.

That's why the Prophet ﷺ said:

من لم يدع قول الزور والعمل به فليس لله حاجة في أن يدع طعامه وشرابه

If one does not avoid lies and false conduct, Allah has no need that he should abstain from his food and his drink. (Bukhari)

The voluntary fasts are weekly and monthly besides the specific voluntary fasts such as the fasts of A'shūra and Muharram. The weekly fasts are twice a week, Mondays and Thursdays and the Monthly ones are three days of every lunar month. These three days are best to be kept in the middle of the month, so the 13th 14th and 15th are recommended.

Aisha صلى says:

كان النبي صلى الله عليه وسلم يتحرَّى صوم الاثنين والخميس

The Prophet صلى الله عليه وسلم was keen to fast Mondays and Thursdays. (Nasai)

وعن أبي أبا ذر رضي الله عنه قال : قال لي رسول الله صلى الله عليه وسلم : إذا صمتَ شيئا من الشهر فصم ثلاث عشرة ، وأربع عشرة ، وخمس عشرة

It was narrated that Abu Dharr صلى said: "The Messenger of Allah صلى الله عليه وسلم said to me, 'If you fast any part of the month then fast on the thirteenth, fourteenth and fifteenth [days].'" (Nasai)

When you are fasting, because you are training your eyes, your ears, your tongue and other parts of your body to obedience to the commands of Allah, then this training will eliminate the whispers of Shaitan when you stand up for Salah. Because throughout the day you were in control of your eyes, you didn't see anything haram, you didn't listen to anything haram, you didn't speak any evil or

Obstructions

85

wrong with your tongue. After spending your day in the obedience of Allah, when you stand before Allah, you will stand with humility and submissiveness fearing Allah, and the voluntary fasts will have become a means to eliminating the whispers of Shaitan in your Salah.

Having Good Manners, Good Character and being Humble

Some people worship Allah and they pay so much attention to worshipping Allah that they don't care about their relationship with the creation of Allah. Unfortunately, some people don't think that having a good character is part of our religion. Some worshippers may have a good relationship with Allah, but their relationship with the creation of Allah is not so good.

The teachings of our religion tell us that if you have excellent ibadah (worship), but terrible akhlaq (manners/character), your ibadah will not make up for the deficiency in your character. On the other hand, if you have excellent akhlaq and decent ibadah, your excellent akhlaq <u>may</u> make up for the deficiency in your ibadah. The proof for this statement is the Hadith about a person came to the Prophet ﷺ, and said "O Messenger of Allah":

امْرَأَةٌ تَصُومُ النَّهَارَ، وَتَقُومُ اللَّيْلَ، وَتُؤْذِي جِيرَانَهَا بِلِسَانِهَا، قَالَ لا خَيْرَ فِيهَا، هِيَ فِي النَّارِ، وَقِيلَ فَامْرَأَةٌ تُصَلِّي الْمَكْتُوبَةَ، وَتَصَدَّقُ مِنْ أَثْوَارِ الأَقِطِ، وَلا تُؤْذِي أَحَدًا بِلِسَانِهَا، قَالَ: هِيَ فِي الْجَنَّةِ

"A certain woman stands up for prayer at night and fasts during the day, and does many a good thing and gives money for charity but she offends her neighbours by what she says." He said: "She is not a good person. She is one of the people of the fire." They said: "A certain woman prays only obligatory prayers and gives little for charity but she does not offend anyone." The Prophet said: "She is one of the people of heaven." (Ahmed)

This shows the importance of having good character over doing voluntary good deeds. It is not possible for a person to harm others with his tongue, with his bad character, and then stand up for Salah and have Khushū' in his Salah.

And no one can say that they have a good enough character and no longer need to improve. This is simply because having good character is not a static achievement, having good character is an ongoing process, which means that no one can actually say that they no longer need to work on their character, because there is always room for improvement.

There are two things that you need to do in order to build good character, because if you don't build good character and you don't display good character in your dealings with Allah's creation, then it is not possible for you to have Khushū' in your Salah.

The first thing to do is to make Du'a to Allah. The Prophet ﷺ taught us the Du'a for having good character. He ﷺ would make Du'a using the following words:

$$\text{اللَّهُمَّ أَحْسَنْتَ خَلْقِي فَأَحْسِنْ خُلُقِي}$$

O Allah, You have made my outward form beautiful so make my attitude good too. (Ibn Hibban)

The second thing to do is to learn about the character of the Prophet ﷺ and to implement this knowledge in your own life. How he used to talk, how he used to treat his wives, how he would deal with the non-muslims, and so on; because the Prophet ﷺ had the best of characters. The Quran praises His character and says:

$$\text{وَإِنَّكَ لَعَلَىٰ خُلُقٍ عَظِيمٍ}$$

And thou (standest) on an exalted standard of character. (Quran [1] 68:4)

Obstructions

Therefore, learning about the character of the Prophet ﷺ and following it, will straighten your relationship with the creation of Allah and will result in helping you to develop Khushū' in your Salah.

Contrary to this, if you don't have a good character, and you harm others with your tongue, with your hands and so on, then how can you expect to stand in Salah with Khushū' when you harm others with that very same tongue?

The Prophet ﷺ was so humble that he spoke softly and was always gentle. He stood for Salah in a state of humility with the highest level of Khushū'. Compare this to a person who is arrogant, always very loud and harsh in character. When he stands in his Salah, how much genuine humility do you think he will have in his Salah?

Therefore, constantly make Du'a to Allah, and build good character by imitating the character of the Prophet ﷺ through studying his biography.

First Things First

There is no deed that will bring a person closer to Allah than those which He has made obligatory upon us. Some people hasten to do voluntary acts but neglect the obligatory acts and get their priorities wrong. Allah said by means of the Prophet ﷺ in the Hadith Qudsi:

وما تقرب إلي عبدي بشيء أحب إلي مما افترضت عليه

My servant does not come closer to Me with anything more dear to Me than that which I made obligatory upon him. (Bukhari)

There is nothing that will bring a person closer to Allah after worshipping Him than serving his parents. Allah commands His servants to be good and kind to their parents immediately after the command to worship Him. He says:

وَقَضَىٰ رَبُّكَ أَلَّا تَعْبُدُوا إِلَّا إِيَّاهُ وَبِالْوَالِدَيْنِ إِحْسَانًا

Your Lord has decreed that you worship none but Him, and do good to parents. (Qur'an [2] 17:23)

Be good to your parents, be kind to them when they attain old age. When you address them be softly spoken to them, fulfil their needs, be respectful and hold on to their feet because that is where you will find Paradise.

Serving your parents must be given greater priority than any other voluntary act. Never let Shaitan whisper you into paying more attention to the voluntary acts whilst neglecting the obligatory acts.

A person came from Yemen came to the Prophet ﷺ and said to him:

أتيت من اليمن أبايعك على الهجرة والجهاد، قال: أحيٌّ والداك؟
قال: نعم. قال:فارجع إلى والديك فأحسن صحبتهما

"O Messenger of Allah! I shall give you my pledge of allegiance to migrate and strive in the cause of Allah."
Upon hearing that, the Prophet ﷺ asked the man: "Are your parents alive?" The man said: "Yes."
He said: "Then go back to your parents and be the best and kindest companion to them." (Muslim)

Ponder and reflect over this Hadith: this person migrated from Yemen to be in the company of the Prophet ﷺ. He left his family, he left his parents, to elevate the religion of Allah with the Prophet ﷺ. The Prophet ﷺ sent him back and said, 'If you seek the reward from Allah then go back to your parents and be as good as you can be to them.'

Never undervalue the obligatory actions compared to the voluntary

Obstructions

actions. And the act that will bring a person closest to Allah after worshipping Him, is kindness to parents.

Every moment you spend with your parents, put a smile on their face, alleviate and eliminate their loneliness by spending time with them. How many are the hearts of parents that suffer thirst and grief, but their thirst is quenched and their grief disappears upon seeing their sons and daughters.

When the Prophet's son, Ibrahim, passed away, he wept ﷺ. When the Companions questioned him about his weeping, he told them it is mercy from Allah. So parents have love, care, affection and mercy for their children. They don't like to see their children struggling and suffering hardships, so though they allow you to go and work, or study etc, be wise and be intelligent with your choices because your parents are in need of you when they are aged and grow weak.

Fear Allah with regard to your parents, and never think when you serve them that you are doing them a favour. No, they are doing you a favour, because by serving them, you are preparing your place in Paradise. Your Paradise lies in serving your parents.

Whilst serving them, if you find them degrading you or using foul language towards you or not appreciating your efforts to help them, continue being good and kind to them, the wisdom behind this may be that Allah wants to increase your status as long as you continue being righteous towards them.

وَإِنْ جَاهَدَاكَ عَلَىٰ أَنْ تُشْرِكَ بِي مَا لَيْسَ لَكَ بِهِ عِلْمٌ فَلَا تُطِعْهُمَا ۖ وَصَاحِبْهُمَا فِي الدُّنْيَا مَعْرُوفًا

However, if they force you to ascribe partners to Me about whom you (can) have no (source of) knowledge, then do not obey them. Remain with them in this world with due fairness, (Quran [2] 31:15)

Diseases of the heart that prevent Khushū'

When you are intending to travel to a third world country, or a developing country, one of the first things that would come to your mind are the diseases in that country. You would be so concerned that you would make sure before you travel that you take the necessary vaccinations to protect you from any kind of infectious disease. You would also make sure that your family members have the necessary inoculations. You would be concerned because you don't want any kind of avoidable illnesses affecting you or your family.

Similarly, there are diseases of the heart, which (if no preventative measures are taken) may corrupt the heart. On the Day of Judgement, neither wealth nor children will benefit one who comes to Allah with an unsound heart. Allah says:

$$\text{يَوْمَ لَا يَنْفَعُ مَالٌ وَلَا بَنُونَ – إِلَّا مَنْ أَتَى اللَّهَ بِقَلْبٍ سَلِيمٍ}$$

The Day when neither wealth will be of any use (to any one) nor sons, Except to him who will come to Allah with a sound heart.
(Quran [2] 88-89)

There are many diseases of the heart, but there are certain ones that will prevent you from developing Khushū' in your Salah. And until you get rid of those diseases, they will continue preventing you from developing Khushū' in your Salah.

The reason why knowing these diseases and their cures is really important is because only by being aware of them will you be on guard against them. And the more aware of them you are, the more you will try to protect yourself from these diseases. It is only by knowing how dangerous it is to drive a car at a high speed that you will make sure to abide by the speed limit.

Obstructions

Having a sound heart is important because the soundness of your body depends upon the soundness of your heart. The Prophet ﷺ said:

أَلَا وَإِنَّ فِي الجَسَدِ مُضْغَةً إِذَا صَلَحَتْ صَلَحَ الجَسَدُ كُلُّهُ وإِذَا فَسَدَت فَسَدَ الجَسَدُ كُلُّهُ أَلَا وَهِيَ القَلْبُ

Indeed there is a piece of flesh in your body which, if it be sound, then the whole body will be sound and if it be corrupt then the whole body will be corrupt. Indeed it is the heart. (Bukhari)

We are not going to mention all the diseases of the heart here, because it would take us beyond the scope of this book, but there are certain diseases that specifically hinder the growth of Khushū', and they will be our focus here.

Before moving further, we must bear in mind that the soundness of the heart is a matter that is in the hands of Allah. Allah is the changer of hearts, and there is no one who can make the heart sound except for Allah. One of the Du'as of the Prophet ﷺ is:

اللهم يا مقلب القلوب ، ثبت قلبي على دينك

O Turner of the hearts, make my heart steadfast in adhering to Your religion. (Tirmidhi)

Given that Allah is the changer of hearts, then there is no better cure for any of the diseases of the heart than by making Du'a to Allah and asking Him to make our hearts steadfast in adhering to His religion.

Pride and Arrogance

Amongst the diseases of the heart that prevents Khushū' is when there is pride or or arrogance in a heart. Firstly, let me clarify the meaning of Pride and Arrogance. Pride and Arrogance is not when someone wears nice clothes, drives a new car or lives in a big mansion. The Prophet ﷺ said:

الكبر بطر الحق وغمط الناس

> Arrogance means rejecting the truth and looking down on people. (Muslim)

In the context of Salah, to assume that my Salah is better than the Salah of my neighbours or that I have more Khushū' in my Salah, or I look down on other people's Salah: these are all considered to be pride and arrogance.

Pride and arrogance are amongst the most severe diseases of the heart. They do not enter any of your acts of worship without destroying it. That is why it is really important to learn the etiquette of worship from the Quran and the Hadith of the Prophet ﷺ. The Quran and the Hadith teach us that one of the fundamentals of worshipping Allah is realizing His greatness in your heart, and that Allah is not in need of your worship. That is why Allah says in the Quran:

لَنْ يَنَالَ اللَّهَ لُحُومُهَا وَلَا دِمَاؤُهَا وَلَكِنْ يَنَالُهُ التَّقْوَىٰ مِنْكُمْ

> It is not their meat nor their blood that reaches Allah: it is your piety that reaches Him. (Quran [1] 22:37)

When you pray Salah or do any other act of worship, bear in mind the greatness of Allah through His names and attributes, that the ability to do this act is a gift to you from Allah, and that you are not doing Allah any favour by offering Salah: it is Allah who is doing you the favour. There are people who worship the sun, the moon, the stars, idols and many other things, but Allah has chosen you to stand before Him. He has not chosen these others, He has favoured you. Such reflection will make you more grateful to Allah for including you amongst the worshippers of the Creator rather than the creation.

Obstructions

When you stand up for Salah, you thank Allah for including you amongst those who worship Him. 'O Allah, I thank you. O Allah, I am grateful to you.' Reflecting in this way will remove any pride and arrogance from your heart.

How can you have pride and arrogance when you were misguided and Allah is the one who guided you? How can you have pride and arrogance when you were poor and Allah is the one who gave you wealth? How can you have pride and arrogance when you were nothing and Allah is the one who gave you the faculty of hearing and seeing? How can you be proud and arrogant before Allah?

So you must realize that YOU are in need of Allah, and YOU are misguided unless Allah guides you, and that YOU cannot live a moment without Allah, no matter how much you worship Him. That is why the Prophet ﷺ said:

لَا يَدْخُلُ أَحَدُكُمُ الْجَنَّةَ بِعَمَلِهِ " قَالُوا: وَلَا أَنْتَ يَا رَسُولَ اللهِ؟ قَالَ: "
وَلَا أَنَا، إِلَّا أَنْ يَتَغَمَّدَنِي اللهُ مِنْهُ بِرَحْمَةٍ وَفَضْلٍ

"No one of you will enter Paradise by his deeds alone." They asked, "Not even you, O Messenger of Allah?" He said, "Not even me, unless Allah covers me with His Grace and Mercy." (Bukhari)

We are reliant upon the mercy of Allah, so how can anyone have pride and arrogance in his heart? I swear by Allah, if all the mountains were made of gold and silver and you spent it all in the path of Allah, it would not suffice as worship of Allah in the way He ought to be worshipped.

That is why when a person has pride and arrogance in his worship he is destroyed. Iblees was amongst the closest to Allah, when he showed pride and arrogance he became one of the losers. How did he become arrogant? He said, "I am better than Adam ﷺ. You created me from fire and You created him from dust." The

94

statement 'I am better' is a statement of pride and arrogance.

Therefore a believer, when worshipping Allah, must worship Him between hope and fear. When you are hoping for Allah's mercy and fearing His punishment there is no room for pride and arrogance at all.

Showing Off

Another disease of the heart is showing off your good deeds. You pray Salah and you show off, for instance, by beautifying your recitation or prolonging your standing or prostration to show off the excellence of your Salah to others. This is a very dangerous disease of the heart because the Prophet ﷺ considered showing off a form of minor or hidden shirk. He ﷺ said:

ألا أخبركم بما هو أخوف عليكم عندي من المسيح الدجال فقلنا بلى يا رسول الله! قال الشرك الخفي أن يقوم الرجل فيصلي فيزين صلاته لما يرى من نظر الرجل

"Shall I not inform you of what I fear for you more than the Masih ad-Dajjal?" They said, "Yes O Messenger of Allah!" He said, "It is the hidden shirk. It is when a man stands up for prayer, then beautifies his prayer for another to look at." (Musnad Ahmed)

The reason why this is called hidden shirk in the Hadith is because the person is doing a religious deed, but he is showing off his good deeds to people and Allah is aware of his intention. Allah knows that this person is not doing this deed for Him, he is doing it for the attention of others. That is why it is called hidden shirk because the person hides his intention in his heart.

The cure for this disease is the same as the above for pride and arrogance: First, by making Du'a to Allah, because He is the turner of the hearts. Second, by realizing who Allah is, knowing Allah by

His names and attributes, knowing that you are not doing a favour to Allah, it is Allah who is doing a favour to you. This realization will eliminate and reduce any kind of showing off from your deeds and make your deeds purely for the sake of Allah.

Laziness

Laziness is amongst the diseases of the heart. A person praying Salah and feeling lazy whilst praying leads to a Salah without Khushū'. And a Salah without Khushū' is nothing but empty movements.

The cure for laziness is realizing the value of Salah. The more you realize the value of Salah the less lazy you will be in your Salah. If I told you that there was 1 million pounds which would be given to you if you were to stand for 24 hours without feeling lazy or drowsy, just for standing on your own two feet...do you think you would stand lazily? I doubt it!

If this is the case for a worldly reward, then how should you be when you are dealing with Allah, the King of all kings; the One Who when He gives, no one can stop Him, and if He were to stop something from you no one can give it to you. All laziness will be removed from you when you remind yourself of Allah's promises to you.

How can you feel lazy standing before Allah, whilst knowing that you are dealing with the King of all kings and the Lord of the worlds?

How can you feel lazy when standing before Allah, whilst reciting the book of Allah, the Quran and knowing that the angels are listening to your recitation?

How can you feel lazy whilst reciting the best speech on the face of this earth, the Quran in which there is news of what happened before you, and information about what is to come after you, a book which will shake your heart and cause you to shed tears?

You feel lazy, because you have not realized who Allah is. You have not realized the status of your standing. You stand in Salah but you don't realize that Allah is watching you, listening to you.

If only you knew what you are reciting whilst reciting the book of Allah. If only you knew who you are dealing with. If only you knew the status and the value of that night that you spent standing before Allah, whilst you were reciting the book of Allah.

Do you not know that the angels descend because you are in the middle of a righteous deed? This recitation of yours is a means to raise your status and achieve forgiveness of your sins.

When you start your Salah and you are standing in front of Allah, without laziness, without showing off, with sincerity, only to please your Lord, without pride or arrogance, then the outcome of this Salah is that you return from your Salah like the day your mother gave birth to you with all your sins forgiven.

O, you who stand in prayer, fear Allah, and know that Allah knows what you hide in your heart; fill your heart with the greatness of Allah and with fear of Him: you will enter the ranks of the righteous people.

Finally, you become lazy due to sin and heedlessness. The cure for both of these diseases is abundance of forgiveness and sincere repentance. In your Du'as ask Allah and say:

اللهم لا تحرمني خير ماعندك بشر ماعندي

O Allah Do not deprive me of the best which is with You, because of the evil within me.

What to do when you get tired during Salah

A common complaint that we hear from many people is that they get tired during Salah. If you get tired during Salah, when reciting the Quran or whilst making Du'a then the best thing to do is to stop

Obstructions

your act of worship and take some rest; this is the Sunnah, because the Prophet ﷺ said:

إِذَا نَعَسَ أَحَدُكُمْ وَهُوَ يُصَلِّي فَلْيَرْقُدْ حَتَّى يَذْهَبَ عَنْهُ النَّوْمُ، فَإِنَّ أَحَدَكُمْ إِذَا صَلَّى وَهُوَ نَاعِسٌ لاَ يَدْرِي لَعَلَّهُ يَسْتَغْفِرُ فَيَسُبَّ نَفْسَهُ

If anyone of you becomes drowsy whilst he is praying, let him sleep until he is refreshed, because if any one of you prays whilst he is drowsy he may not understand what he is saying and he may mean to pray for forgiveness, but may insult himself by mistake instead. (Bukhari)

Al-Nawawi said: "this is general and applies to both obligatory and to naafil prayers offered at night and during the day. This is our view and the view of the majority. But he should not delay an obligatory prayer until the time for it is over." (Al Majmoo)

Tiredness can be broadly categorised into two types. The first is genuine tiredness, whereby a person may not have had a full rest due to work, study or other household responsibilities and he is physically tired. For such a person it is better for him to take some rest and then continue with his worship.

The second type of tiredness is when you have had all the rest that your body requires, but yet, when you stand up for Salah you are weary, you feel drowsy and lethargic, and you stand in Salah sluggishly. When you experience this, then you must realize that this type of tiredness is from Shaitan. This is a sign of weak Iman and lack of awareness of Allah. One does not realize that one is standing before Allah. One enjoys all of the blessings of Allah and His favours upon oneself and upon one's family and children, but when the time comes to stand before Allah, one feels tired and sleepy.

The cure for this type of tiredness is to follow the 8 practical steps which are outlined in the next section of this book.

ACTIONS

Actions

A Muslim once entered a hotel in France, at the time of Salah, and he wanted to know the direction of the Qiblah. So he asked a man he saw in the hotel, "Excuse me, are you a Muslim?" "I am a Muslim, I am a Sunni, and I am a Maliki (i.e. a follower of the Maliki school of fiqh)." "Ok, which direction is the Qiblah?" "I don't know, I don't pray Salah."

If what you believe in has no impact on how you behave, then what you believe in is not important. We can say nice things about developing Khushū', but unless we put it into action, it just remains nice words: of no value whatsoever. Similarly, until you put these suggestions into action, your desire to develop Khushū' is only a fantasy.

Once you have got rid of the obstructions and barriers that are preventing you from developing Khushū' in your Salah, it is time to move on to the third phase of the 'Threefold Method': the Actions. Actions are the things that you must do and put into practice if you want your Salah to give you peace of mind and coolness of the eyes.

The list of these actions have been simplified for you so as to make it easy for you to remember them, using the acronym 'PARADISE'.

With each of these eight concepts, I am going to help you, step-by-step. I have broken it down for you to show you how you can develop Khushū' in your Salah by following each step in this model, *as long as you put them into action*. I suggest and advise you not to skip a single one of these steps, because each one is a precious diamond, such that even if you master only one of them, it will make a huge difference to your Khushū'.

Therefore, please find a place to read these steps where you can be alone and uninterrupted. Clear your mind of everything, except what you are about to read and what I invite you to do. Don't worry about your schedule, your business, your family, or your friends. Just focus with me and open your mind. You cannot afford to be distracted because I am going to share valuable pearls and treasures with you that will develop Khushū' in your Salah: and this is exactly the reason why you have this book in your hand.

Actions

'8 Steps of Actions'

8 Steps for developing Khushū' in Salah

P	**Preparation**
A	**Awareness**
R	**Recitation**
A	**Arabic**
D	**Dua**
I	**Imagination**
S	**Stance**
E	**Eternal Life**

Actions for building Khushū' that may not work

You may find some people who try many things to develop Khushū' in their Salah, but they are not successful. For example, some people try developing Khushū' by closing their eyes; some try by humbling their bodies more than their hearts; some try turning off the lights. These will be discussed later on in the book in their appropriate sections; but I want to draw your attention here to something that is important, and that is: any method that is not from the Quran and the Hadith does not work. The method for developing Khushū' must be taken from the Quran and the Hadith, because there is no one better qualified to show us the path for developing Khushū' than Allah and His Messenger ﷺ. Adopting methods from sources other than the Quran and the Hadith (and thus not approved by Allah and His Messenger ﷺ), no matter how good they may appear to be, they are not going to work.

Authenticity

Therefore, in this book, what we have done is to take all the methods and steps from Quran and the Hadith. That is why if you implement any one of the steps, even if they do not work for you in your development of Khushū', you will still be rewarded because there is always benefit in following the teachings of Allah and His Messenger ﷺ. However, as long as you follow the steps I am going to share with you, - if Allah wills - they will help you to develop Khushū' in your Salah.

Actions

P A R A D I S E

P is for . . . Preparation

When you plan to do anything, even as small as cooking a meal, don't you go to the shops to gather the ingredients? Don't you prepare the ingredients before you cook your food?

When you are learning to cook and you are still a novice, it will take you longer to prepare it than it would if you were to cook on a daily basis. When you become used to preparing your food every day, after a week or ten days it will become so easy for you that it doesn't feel like a burden anymore when preparing it.

You may be asking yourself: 'Why is he giving me this cooking metaphor?' Well, it is because we learn two things here. The first thing we learn is that preparation is vital, without it you may not succeed. If the foundation of a building is not prepared well, the structure of the building will not be strong and solid, and will fail its inspection. Therefore, preparation is vital.

The second thing that we learn is that once you do something regularly, no matter how difficult it may be initially, by constant and regular practice this task will become second nature to you. You will then do the task without even thinking about it, simply because you are now accustomed to it.

These two points apply just as well to the preparation of your Salah. Never think that it is not important: as we have just illustrated, we need to give thought and effort to something as simple as food preparation. That being true, how can you not prepare for your Salah, the righteous deed of worshipping Allah?

Second, never think that because Salah has been made compulsory to pray five times a day, that we need to spend a great deal of time preparing **FIVE** times a day. For many people this seems like a big problem, which results in them not preparing for their Salah at all.

But remember, just like when preparing the food, after 7-10 days, it will become second nature: you won't think of it as preparing food even though that is what you are doing. This is because when you do something every day, it becomes routine. Similarly, when you prepare five times a day for your Salah, within 3-5 days your preparation for Salah will become second nature to you and you will become used to it.

Now that you understood these two points, you can see how vital the first step of Action of 'preparation' is. There are three things that you must do when you are preparing for your Salah. These are the ingredients for the preparation of your Salah, but you won't need to buy them from any shop. I am going to share them with you right here, so just grab them and put them into action beginning with your next Salah. Don't delay, act now!

1 – The Missing Ingredients

No one would disagree on the obligation of being in the state of Wudhu before praying Salah. The question is, why does it not prepare you for Salah, in the way it prepared the righteous predecessors?

If you were to read their stories and how their state would change whilst performing Wudhu, you will realize that even though you may be doing the same things in Wudhu that they did, there is something that is missing in our Wudhu which was always present in theirs.

When Imam Ali Zaynul Abideen (رحمة الله عليه) would perform Wudhu, the colour of his face would change and become pale. Somebody asked him the reason for that and he said: "Don't you know before whom I am going to stand? I am going to stand before my Lord and my Creator."

The missing ingredient is that of reflection and contemplation. So long as you fail to understand the greatness of the Wudhu that you are performing, it will be difficult for you to reach the state that they reached.

So the question is: How do I attain this missing ingredient? The answer is by going back to the Quran and the Hadith, because that is the place where we will find the missing ingredient.

The Quran and the Prophet ﷺ enlighten us as to the rewards, virtues and the greatness of Wudhu, and when you reflect upon these statements, it will instil that missing ingredient into your Wudhu. This can be done when you ponder and reflect on the following virtues of Wudhu. Pondering over them will take your Wudhu to the next level.

Wudhu is a Means to Allah loving you

Allah says in the Quran:

$$إِنَّ اللَّهَ يُحِبُّ التَّوَّابِينَ وَيُحِبُّ الْمُتَطَهِّرِينَ$$

Surely Allah loves those who are most repenting, and loves those who keep themselves pure (and clean).
(Quran [2] 2:222)

Wudhu is a Means to the acceptance of Du'a

The Prophet ﷺ said:

$$ما من مسلم يبيت على ذكر طاهرا فيتعار من الليل فيسأل الله خيرا$$
$$من الدنيا والآخرة إلا أعطاه إياه$$

If a Muslim sleeps while remembering Allah, in the state of purification, is alarmed while asleep at night, and asks Allah for good in this world and in the Hereafter. He surely gives it to him. (Abu Dawood)

Wudhu is a Means to the forgiveness of Sins

The Prophet ﷺ said:

مَنْ تَوَضَّأَ فَأَحْسَنَ الْوُضُوءَ خَرَجَتْ خَطَايَاهُ مِنْ جَسَدِهِ حَتَّى تَخْرُجَ مِنْ تَحْتِ أَظْفَارِهِ

He who performs the Wudhu perfectly (i.e., according to the Sunnah), his sins will depart from his body, even from under his nails. (Muslim)

In another Hadith the Prophet ﷺ said:

إِذَا تَوَضَّأَ الْعَبْدُ الْمُسْلِمُ أَوِ الْمُؤْمِنُ فَغَسَلَ وَجْهَهُ خَرَجَ مِنْ وَجْهِهِ كُلُّ خَطِيئَةٍ نَظَرَ إِلَيْهَا بِعَيْنَيْهِ مَعَ الْمَاءِ أَوْ مَعَ آخِرِ قَطْرِ الْمَاءِ فَإِذَا غَسَلَ يَدَيْهِ خَرَجَ مِنْ يَدَيْهِ كُلُّ خَطِيئَةٍ كَانَ بَطَشَتْهَا يَدَاهُ مَعَ الْمَاءِ أَوْ مَعَ آخِرِ قَطْرِ الْمَاءِ فَإِذَا غَسَلَ رِجْلَيْهِ خَرَجَتْ كُلُّ خَطِيئَةٍ مَشَتْهَا رِجْلَاهُ مَعَ الْمَاءِ أَوْ مَعَ آخِرِ قَطْرِ الْمَاءِ حَتَّى يَخْرُجَ نَقِيًّا مِنَ الذُّنُوبِ

When a Muslim, or a believer, washes his face (in the course of Wudhu), every sin which he committed with his eyes, will be washed away from his face with the water, or with the last drop of water; when he washes his hands, every sin which is committed by his hands will be effaced from his hands with the water, or with the last drop of water; and when he washes his feet, every sin his feet committed will be washed away with the water, or with the last drop of water; until he finally emerges cleansed of all his sins. (Muslim)

Wudhu is a Means of elevation in the ranks of Paradise

The Prophet ﷺ said:

أَلَا أَدُلُّكُمْ عَلَى مَا يَمْحُو اللَّهُ بِهِ الْخَطَايَا وَيَرْفَعُ بِهِ الدَّرَجَاتِ قَالُوا بَلَى يَا رَسُولَ اللَّهِ. قَالَ : إِسْبَاغُ الْوُضُوءِ عَلَى الْمَكَارِهِ وَكَثْرَةُ الْخُطَا إِلَى الْمَسَاجِدِ وَانْتِظَارُ الصَّلَاةِ بَعْدَ الصَّلَاةِ فَذَلِكُمُ الرِّبَاطُ

"Shall I not tell you something by which Allah effaces the sins and elevates ranks (in Paradise)?" The Companions said; "Certainly, O Messenger of Allah." He ﷺ said, "Performing Wudhu thoroughly in spite of difficult circumstances, walking a long distance to the mosque, and waiting there for the next Salat (prayer) after observing the previous one; and that is Ar-Ribat," (Muslim)

Ar-Ribat means watching the frontiers or battlefront to check the invasion of the enemy. Performing Wudhu thoroughly in spite of difficult circumstances is regarded as Ribat for the reason that by so doing, such a person is constantly engaged in the obedience and worship of Allah to keep Shaitan away from him.

Now try doing Wudhu!

How can you do Wudhu without Khushū' after knowing that whilst you wash your limbs, Allah loves you because you are keeping yourself clean and pure?

How can you do Wudhu without Khushū' after knowing that whilst you wash your limbs, your sins are being forgiven and your rank is being raised in Paradise?

The next time that you do Wudhu, call these virtues and their greatness to your mind and heart and then go ahead. I can assure you that the difference between doing Wudhu without awareness of these virtues and then doing it after discovering them and bearing them in mind on every occasion is great: your Wudhu will be on a completely different level. Try it, and see the difference!

There is a world of difference between doing Wudhu without recalling these virtues and doing it mindfully with them. This is the reason why these Hadiths are there, to trigger this recollection in your heart when you do Wudhu.

These missing ingredients in Wudhu are so important that *not* having them could simply mean that your heart will always be distracted by worldly matters during Wudhu. This is not appropriate because you are preparing and washing yourself to stand before your Lord, you are preparing to call on Him, to speak to Him, to hope for His mercy and to fear His punishment.

That is why the Khushū' of the pious predecessors began with their Wudhu. They would anticipate the sweetness of Salah whilst doing Wudhu, whilst pouring the cold water in winter, whilst getting out of their warm beds for Fajr; that is the place where they would feel the sweetness of worship, because they would recall the reward and the promises that Allah has made to the believers in the Quran and in the Hadith.

For people who were on the highest level of Khushū', the place where their Khushū' of Salah began was in preparing for Salah. This is exactly the place where I want you to be: at the highest level of Khushū'.

2 – The value of your steps to the Masjid

Do you know how valuable your steps are as you walk towards the Masjid? The Prophet ﷺ said:

بشر المشائين في الظلم إلى المساجد بالنور التام يوم القيامة

"Announce good news to those walking to the Mosques in darkness (for the morning and the night prayers) that they will have radiant light on the Day of Judgment." (Abu Dawood).

He ﷺ said:

من غدا إلى المسجد أو راح، أعد الله له في الجنة نزلا كلما غدا أو
راح

"Whoever heads for the Mosque in the morning or evening, Allah prepares for him a reward in Paradise for each time he walks to the Mosque." (Bukhari and Muslim).

He ﷺ said:

من تطهر في بيته، ثم مضى إلى بيت من بيوت الله، ليقضي فريضة من فرائض الله، كانت خطواته، إحداها تحط خطيئة، والأخرى ترفع درجة

"Whoever purified (did Wudhu) himself in his house, and then walked to one of the Houses of Allah (Masjid) to perform an obligatory Salah, each of his footsteps marks the alternation between the subtraction of a sin and the addition of a reward." (Muslim)

Let me ask you: When was the last time you walked to the Masjid and reflected upon every step that you took there as a reward when you raised your feet and forgiveness of a sin when you lowered your feet?

When was the last time you walked to the Masjid and pondered every time you walked upon Allah preparing a reward for you in Paradise?

When was the last time you walked to the Masjid and reflected every time you walked in darkness (for the morning and the night prayers) upon the radiant light that you will have on the Day of Judgment?

These reflections will help to prepare you for developing Khushū' in your Salah. Reflect on the fact the Allah has chosen you to walk to the Masjid to stand before Him, so you are one of those chosen by Allah to stand before Him. Reflect on the fact that Allah has blessed you.

Do you know when will you appreciate this? When you see those around you who have not been given the opportunity by Allah to stand before Him. The time when you see during your walk to the Masjid the people around you who are engaged in the pleasures of this world, with their magazines, on the Internet, with their Facebook page and WhatsApp; and you have thrown behind you all of these distractions to stand before Him because He has chosen you to stand before Him.

These reflections will prepare you to develop Khushū' in your Salah. They will give you the sweetness of worship, the coolness of your eyes whilst walking; and the inconvenience that you experience in walking towards the Masjid will begin to feel agreeable, a comfort and a relief. This is exactly the feeling I want you to experience when you walk to the Masjid, because this is what the pious predecessors experienced in the apparent discomfort of preparing to worship Allah.

Do not run whilst going to Pray

Do not run or hurry in your walk when approaching Salah, instead walk with calmness and with respect. As the Prophet ﷺ said:

إِذَا سَمِعْتُمُ الإِقَامَةَ فَامْشُوا إِلَى الصَّلَاةِ، وَعَلَيْكُمْ بِالسَّكِينَةِ وَالْوَقَارِ وَلاَ تُسْرِعُوا، فَمَا أَدْرَكْتُمْ فَصَلُّوا وَمَا فَاتَكُمْ فَأَتِمُّوا

"When you hear the Iqama, proceed to offer the prayer with calmness and solemnity and do not make haste. And pray whatever you are able to pray and complete whatever you have missed." (Bukhari)

3 – The Secret of Allahu Akbar

This step in the preparation is such an important one, that even if you only do this one step properly, you will greatly increase the Khushū' in your Salah. If you do nothing else, just doing this one step properly, (i.e. the way I am going to explain it to you,) will take your Salah to a completely different level – if Allah wills –.

Allahu Akbar means 'Allah is the Greatest'. When you raise your hands whilst saying the takbir (Allahu Akbar), then here is what you need to reflect upon:

Put all your worries, anxieties, problems, sadness, and all the worldly problems that you can think of, in short everything and everyone, balance them on the back of your hands and as you raise them towards your ears, imagine that you are throwing all of these worldly matters behind you, and that there is nothing in your heart, in your mind, in your soul greater than Allah.

The secret of implementing this step is that throughout your Salah, whoever comes or whatever comes in your Salah, you have prepared yourself pondering the greatness of Allah. Therefore, it is insignificant for any other thing to present itself to you in your Salah.

If your phone rings, you hear a knock on the door or someone comes: do not interrupt your Salah, because you are standing before the King of all kings, who is greater than all of these worldly matters that are trying to disturb you. At any time or moment, for any distraction entering your Salah, eradicate it by reflecting on this secret and the wisdom behind 'Allahu Akbar'.

When the people of Khushū', the pious predecessors, stood up for Salah, the moment they said 'Allahu Akbar', all the concerns of the world became insignificant to them.

The reason why Allah has made the opening of the Salah 'Allahu Akbar', is so that we realize that there is nothing in my heart, there is nothing in my mind, and there is nothing in my soul greater than Allah. Because when we believe in the insignificance of everything in this world compared to His greatness, it becomes disgraceful to be thinking about our cars, spouses, children and so on, whilst standing before the Almighty.

The Prophet ﷺ said:

إِنَّ الرَّجُلَ لَيَنْصَرِفُ وَمَا كُتِبَ لَهُ إِلَّا عُشْرُ صَلَاتِهِ، تُسْعُهَا، ثُمُنُهَا،

سُبْعُهَا، سُدُسُهَا، خُمْسُهَا، رُبْعُهَا، ثُلُثُهَا، نِصْفُهَا

"A man may complete the Salah and only have recorded for himself one-tenth or one-ninth or one-eighth or one-seventh or one-fifth or one-fourth or one-third or one-half (of them). (Abu Dawood)

So when you pray Salah, you will only benefit to the level of the Khushū' that you have in your Salah, and the Khushū' that was lost in these short moments is better than this world and everything in it. If you knew the reward and the honour before Allah, then the amount of Khushū' that is lost is more valuable than this world and all it contains.

This shows that everything that is in this world, its glitter and its pleasures, as well as its pains and its difficulties, are insignificant and unworthy to have your focus when your heart needs to be turned to Allah.

Allah tells us in the Quran:

وَاسْتَعِينُوا بِالصَّبْرِ وَالصَّلَاةِ

Seek help through patience and prayer. (Quran [2] 2:45)

The reason why Allah tells us to seek His help through prayer is because when you say 'Allahu Akbar' (Allah is the Greatest), all your worries, anxieties and any worldly problems become insignificant, because Allah is the Greatest.

When you understand the meaning of 'Allahu Akbar', and the wisdom behind raising your hands then how can you be distracted from Khushū'? How can you be drawn to the temptations of this world? When you implement this method and say 'Allah is the Greatest', all of the temptations of this world and desire will dissolve away. This will mean that neither your business, nor your wealth, family, children nor the illness of someone close to you will divert you from Allah, because all of these are insignificant compared to your standing before the Lord of the worlds.

This reflection is so powerful that those who reflect in this way, even if they happen to begin their Salah in a state of sadness and worry, by the end of their Salah every trace of their sadness or preoccupation will have evaporated.

P A R A D I S E

2

A is for . . . Awareness

Having the right sense of awareness is an important step for developing Khushū'. The brain and mind that Allah has given us is unable to focus on two different things 100%. You can focus 80/20 or 60/40 on two different things, but you will never achieve 100% focus on two different things. Therefore, whilst standing for Salah, if the right awareness is not created, your mind's focus will drift to worldly matters, your business, your career, on your children and family.

If you have prepared correctly, and put all worldly matters out of your mind when you said "Allahu Akbar", your mind is free of distractions. It must now be filled with the right awareness in order to keep it from wandering. You need to concentrate simply and solely on your Salah.

I want you to experience the sustainability of Khushū' throughout your Salah, not just for a few moments. If you want continuous Khushū' in your Salah, then you need to pay attention to this step. Implementing this step, following the tips I am going to share with you, will result in sustained Khushū' in your Salah. This will reduce distractions whilst standing before the Almighty. With diligent practice, you will achieve zero distractions, which is exactly what you want.

In order to create the correct sense of awareness in your Salah, you need to have the following three components:

- Awareness of the Greatness of Salah
- Awareness of the Greatness of Allah
- Awareness of who your true friend and enemy is

1 – Awareness of the Greatness of Salah

One reason why Khushū' in your Salah is hard for you to maintain could be that you have lost sight of the grandeur of your Salah. Imagine that you have enrolled in a college course. You start the course and go to your lectures daily, but you don't focus or pay attention to the lecturer. It later transpires that this course would have been instrumental in changing the course of your life and career. Am I right in saying that, had you been aware of this, of having a good career upon its completion, that your focus would have been different in the class? If you had known that successfully completing this course would give you a good job, a long term career, which would have meant a substantial income for you and your family, which would have provided a comfortable life, wouldn't this awareness have changed your attitude in your class?

Similarly, when you become aware of the greatness of Salah, your level of Khushū' will dramatically increase and maintain itself in your Salah.

Don't You Know?

Salah is the best of all deeds.

سئل رسول الله صلى الله عليه وآله وسلم : أي العمل أفضل ؟ قال :
الصلاة في أول وقتها

The Prophet ﷺ was asked, "Which deed is best?" He said, "Prayer in its proper time." (Hakim)

Don't You Know?

Salah is the most beloved deed to Allah.

سئل رسول الله صلى الله عليه وآله وسلم : أي العمل أحب إلى الله ؟
قال : الصلاة في أول وقتها

The Prophet ﷺ was asked, "Which is the most beloved deed to Allah?" He said, "Prayer in its proper time." (Bukhari)

Don't You Know?

Salah was the last advice of the Prophet ﷺ before leaving this world.

كَانَ آخِرُ وَصِيَّةٍ رَسُولِ اللَّهِ صَلَّى اللَّهُ عَلَيْهِ وَآلِهِ وَسَلَّمَ حِينَ حَضَرَهُ الْمَوْتُ" الصَّلَاةَ الصَّلَاةَ "

The Prophet's last advice during his final sickness ﷺ was "Guard your prayers, Guard your prayers." (Hakim)

Don't You Know?

Salah is what differentiates between a Muslim and a Non-Muslim.

بين الكفر والإيمان ترك الصلاة

Salah is the partition between disbelief and faith. (Tirmidhi)

Don't You Know?

There is no excuse to miss Salah upon the non-availability of water.

فَلَمْ تَجِدُوا مَاءً فَتَيَمَّمُوا صَعِيدًا طَيِّبًا

If ... ye find no water, then take for yourselves clean sand or earth, (Quran [1] 5:6)

Don't You Know?

There is no excuse to miss Salah when being unable to stand.

صَلِّ قَائِمًا ، فَإِنْ لَمْ تَسْتَطِعْ فَقَاعِدًا ، فَإِنْ لَمْ تَسْتَطِعْ فَعَلَى جَنْبٍ

Pray standing; if you cannot, then sitting; and if you cannot, then lying on your side. (Bukhari)

Don't You Know?

The Prophet ﷺ went to the heavens and Allah gifted him with this Salah.

Don't You Know?

The first matter that you will be brought to account for on the Day of Judgment is your Salah.

إِنَّ أَوَّلَ مَا يُحَاسَبُ بِهِ الْعَبْدُ يَوْمَ الْقِيَامَةِ مِنْ عَمَلِهِ صَلَاتُهُ

The first thing that the servant will be called to account for on the Day of Judgment will be his Salah. (Abu Dawood, Tirmidhi)

Don't You Know?

Salah keeps you away from evil deeds.

إِنَّ الصَّلَاةَ تَنْهَىٰ عَنِ الْفَحْشَاءِ وَالْمُنْكَرِ

for Prayer restrains from shameful and unjust deeds; (Quran 29:45)

Don't You Know?

Salah is a means for removing all sorts of worries and anxieties and paying of your debts.

يَا أَيُّهَا الَّذِينَ آمَنُوا اتَّقُوا اللَّهَ وَابْتَغُوا إِلَيْهِ الْوَسِيلَةَ وَجَاهِدُوا فِي سَبِيلِهِ لَعَلَّكُمْ تُفْلِحُونَ

O you who believe, fear Allah and seek means of nearness to Him, and carry out Jihad in His way, so that you may succeed. (Quran [2] 5:35)

When you realize and become aware of the greatness of this Salah, many doors of blessings and mercy and goodness can open for you due to this Salah. When you stand before Him, realize that you are enacting one of the best of all deeds. And all that this world contains of its pleasures and luxuries is completely insignificant compared to *this* Salah that you are standing in *now*.

By Allah, never grieve over any loss that you incur in this world, but regret leaving this world and not worshipping Allah the way He ought to be worshipped.

Today a person becomes upset and cries over worldly matters and its pleasures and luxuries, and the calamities in his family, wealth and children. Yet he does not care about the rights of Allah and the duty he owes his Creator. Whereas the pious predecessors, upon missing a Salah, would be in pain and would cry as though they had lost something priceless. Losing anything related to Salah is truly a great loss.

مَنْ فَاتَتْهُ صَلَاةُ الْعَصْرِ فَكَأَنَّمَا وُتِرَ أَهْلُهُ وَمَالُهُ

Whoever misses the Asr prayer (intentionally) then it is as if he lost his family and property. (Bukhari)

When you know how great this Salah is, it will be very difficult for your mind to wander whilst standing before Allah: instead this Salah will become the coolness of your eyes just like the way it was for the pious predecessors.

2 – Awareness of the Greatness of Allah

Imagine that a king has invited you for a meeting with him in his palace. Upon arrival, you are honoured by the king and the meeting commences. Now, what are the chances of your mind wandering whilst you are interacting with this king? I assume it would be highly unlikely.

If I ask you the reason for this, you may say that it is because you

119

are with the king, the ruler of the country. In other words because you have an awareness of this king's importance, it is unlikely that your mind will wander when interacting with him.

When you realize who you are speaking with in your Salah then it will become impossible for your mind to wander.

When you create this awareness of standing before Allah, you are worshipping Him as if you see Him. Though you do not see Him, yet you know that He sees you: with which tongue do you say (الحمد لله

رب العالمين) 'All praise is to Allah the Lord of the worlds'? Because this is not a place where everyone gets the opportunity to stand.

With which tongue do you speak of the mercy of Allah? (الرحمن

الرحيم) 'The Most Gracious the Most Merciful'.

With which tongue do you talk about the Judgement? The master of this day is none other than Allah. (ملك يوم الدين) 'Master of the Day of Judgement'.

With which tongue, with which heart or with which limb do you say (إياك نعبد وإياك نستعين) 'You alone we worship and You alone we ask for help'?

Your heart humbles at that moment, your body humbles at that point because you are standing in an honourable place, and you are standing in a praiseworthy place. Because you are standing before the Only One, the One Who does not beget, nor is He begotten, and there is nothing like unto Him.

On the other hand, when you don't create this awareness of standing before Him, your mind will wander and your Salah is nothing more than mere movements which result in Salah without a soul. And as Ibn Qayyim (رحمة الله عليه) said, "A Salah without a soul is like a body without a soul." What value does a body have without a soul? Similarly, what value does a Salah have without a soul?

In order to create this awareness, there are two things that you need to do. And I am going to share with you exactly what you need to do in order to create this awareness, so that when you stand before Allah your Salah becomes a coolness for your eyes. It will give you so much peace that the moment you use the methods I am going to share with you, all your worries, anxieties and sadness will be replaced with happiness and peace.

The first awareness you need to create is that of knowing Who Allah is and the second is that of knowing what Allah does for you i.e. the awareness of His blessings upon you.

Creating Awareness of Who Allah Is

There is nothing more powerful in creating this awareness than knowing Allah through His names and attributes. Know that Allah is The Most Gracious, The Most Merciful, The Most Perfect, The King, The Source of Peace and Safety. Know that He is the one who created you and shaped you and gave you the senses of hearing and sight. Know that if Allah were to punish men for their sins, He would not leave, on the earth, a single living creature: but He lets them go on up to an appointed time.

When you know Who Allah is, through His names and attributes, and then you recite the Quran, pondering over it, reflecting upon it (how to reflect whilst reciting will be covered in the next section), then you will be gifted with the love of Allah and the fear of Allah. You will love Allah and therefore you will hope for His mercy and you will fear Allah and therefore you will fear His punishment. And both of these are important ingredients in your worship of Allah.

If you had to stand in front of a king of this world, one who cannot benefit nor harm your soul, how would you stand? How about standing before Allah, the One in whose hands is your life and death, the One Who when He decides to benefit you none can harm you, and the One Who when He decides to harm you none can benefit you? When you stand with hope and fear, then Allah will grant you the sweetness of talking to Him, and the happiness of standing before Him, to the level that the Prophet ﷺ said, "the coolness of my eyes lies in Salah". (Ahmed, Nasai) At this point your heart will be humble in your Salah and you too will find the coolness of your eyes in the Salah.

Creating Awareness of His Blessings

The second part of increasing awareness of Allah is by being aware of His blessings upon you.

Every day, Allah showers His blessings and generosity upon you, your family and your children. If you were to count the blessings of Allah, you will never be able to number them. Every morning and evening you are in His protection, in His mercy, in His Grace and in His kindness, yet after all this you are far away from His glorification. This ignorance of Allah is a tragedy.

To create this awareness, ask yourself questions such as, 'Who is the One Who has guided me?' 'Who is the One Who has granted me the ability to stand before Him?' 'Who is the One Who sent messengers to us, and revealed this book (Quran) and guided me?'

You will realize this and you will appreciate the value of this when you see people around you worshipping other than Allah. When you remind yourself of the worshippers of trees, stones and rocks, worshippers of the sun and moon, those who associate partners with Allah which can neither benefit nor harm them; whilst on the other hand, you are directed with the guidance of Allah. At this point you will truly appreciate the blessing of Iman and Islam and standing before Him in Salah.

That is why Ibn Umar ؓ would call unto Allah with the following Du'a on Mount Safa:

اللهم إنك قلت (ادعوني استجب لكم) وإنك لا تخلف الميعاد اللهم
كما هديتني للإسلام فلا تنزعه مني حتى تقبضني وأنا عليه

2

O Allah, You have said, 'call on Me - I will answer you' and
You do not break Your promise. So I am asking You, in the
same way that You have guided me to Islam, not to take it
away from me, and that You let me die as a Muslim.

Creating awareness of the blessings of Allah will maintain your
Khushū' throughout your Salah. Allah pours blessings upon you
every day, in fact, every *moment* of your life, and you enjoy these
blessings. Yet the only thing Allah asks from you is to stand before
Him just five times a day for a few moments? Can you not hold
Khushū' for a few minutes? Can you not stand before Allah for a
few moments reciting the Quran, pondering and reflecting upon it
with Khushū'?

O Allah we complain to you of our weakness: there is no greater
sadness for any person than to leave this world not being amongst
the people of Khushū'; this is a true tragedy for anyone. A person
standing up for Salah, whose body is with him but his heart is
outside of Salah:

إنا لله وإنا إليه راجعون

Surely we belong to Allah and to Him shall we return

3 – Awareness of who your true friend and enemy is

Picture for a moment that you are an employee in a company and
you want to be promoted to a managerial position. But in order to
get to that position you need to excel in your performance, which
means a lot of hard work will probably be necessary. You are
getting advice from two mentors, but their advice is contradictory.
Later on you find out from a reliable source that Mentor A is
envious of you, whereas Mentor B is a loyal and sincere friend to

you. After receiving this information, would you follow Mentor A's advice or Mentor B's advice? Surely, it would be Mentor B's advice, because you have discovered Mentor A's negative feelings towards you. Had you not been made aware of this, you might have followed Advisor A's advice, which could have prevented you from being promoted.

This is exactly what you need to be aware of in your Salah. So long as you remain unaware of who is your enemy and who is your friend, you will continue to be distracted in your Salah. Your enemy is Shaitan and your Protecting Friend is none other than Allah.

Once you reach this stage of awareness, then every time Shaitan whispers, you know that this whisper is from your enemy who does not want you to be 'promoted'. Remember, anything that might prevent you from developing Khushū' in your Salah is from Shaitan, who is always your enemy.

In order to acquire this awareness, you need to find a reliable source explaining who your enemy is and who your friend is. There is no more reliable source than the Quran. Allah tells us in the Quran:

$$\text{إِنَّ الشَّيْطَانَ لَكُمْ عَدُوٌّ فَاتَّخِذُوهُ عَدُوًّا ۚ إِنَّمَا يَدْعُو حِزْبَهُ لِيَكُونُوا مِنْ أَصْحَابِ السَّعِيرِ}$$

Verily Satan is an enemy to you: so treat him as an enemy. He only invites his adherents that they may become Companions of the Blazing Fire. (Quran [1] 35:6)

$$\text{إِنَّمَا وَلِيُّكُمُ اللَّهُ وَرَسُولُهُ وَالَّذِينَ آمَنُوا الَّذِينَ يُقِيمُونَ الصَّلَاةَ وَيُؤْتُونَ الزَّكَاةَ وَهُمْ رَاكِعُونَ}$$

Your (real) friends are [no less than] Allah, His Messenger, and the Believers, those who establish regular prayers and pay charity, and they bow down humbly (in worship).

(Quran [1] 5:55)

In these verses, Allah tells us who our enemy is and who our friends are. Just as you wouldn't take career advice from someone who is envious of you, because he will secretly be working against your chances of promotion; in the same way, not being aware of who your enemy and friends are in your Salah will prevent you from developing Khushū' and from any promotion that will get you closer to Allah.

Allah is the one who will open His doors of mercy for you: Shaitan does not want you to receive any share of Allah's mercy. Shaitan will distract you by whispering. He will remind you of your shopping list for the week, he will remind you of the things that you forgot to do, he will remind you of the things that you need to do; He is an open enemy to you.

This awareness of the enmity of Shaitan will reduce his whispers dramatically, because once you are aware of his enmity, you will be on guard against his whispers or anything that is preventing your development of Khushū' (and anything that prevents Khushū' is from Shaitan) in your Salah between you and your Lord Who is your true Friend.

Note: The method of dealing with the whispers of Shaitan has already been discussed at length in the earlier part of this book. This section is specifically concerned with awareness of the enmity of Shaitan and the friendship of Allah.

P A R A D I S E

R is for . . . Recitation

This is one of the most important steps, because a large portion of your Salah is recitation. When you recite the Quran in Salah, there are two things that are important for you to do to develop your Khushū'. These two things are so important that if they are missing in your recitation then you will be losing out on the sweetness of your Salah.

The two things that you must have when reciting the Quran in Salah are:

1. Reflection and Pondering over the Recitation.
2. Crying during Recitation.

You can either recite the Quran like a story book, or by reflecting and pondering over it, and by interacting with it. What most people do is read the Quran the first way: then they wonder as to why they cannot taste the sweetness of the recitation. When your practice is to read it the first way, you become tired and weary very quickly, which is an obstacle to the development of Khushū'.

I used to wonder how some scholars of the past would recite the Quran without feeling weary or tired. I am not referring here to the small Surahs, but two or three of the longest Surahs in the Quran. Some would even recite the entire Quran in one night without getting tired: they were enjoying the sweetness of the Quranic recitation. If this is what you want to experience, follow the method that I am going to share with you. Put it into action from your next Salah and you will swiftly see the difference!

1 – Recitation without a Spirit

Many of us recite the Quran like reading a book, without understanding or reflecting upon it.

Take Surah Fatihah: if you were to spend days reflecting only on this one Surah you would still only perceive some of its great and magnificent meanings. If you just reflected and pondered over this one Surah alone, though you may enter your Salah worried and distressed, merely by reciting (الحمد لله رب العالمين) [All praise is to Allah the Lord of the worlds] with reflection, pondering on just this one verse, all of your worries and distress would disappear. You could be in a completely different world that cannot be described. As the Prophet ﷺ said:

'The coolness of my eyes lies in the Salah.' (Ahmed, Nasai)

So: What can you do to reflect and ponder over the Quran so that you too can experience the sweetness of Salah as the pious predecessors did?

There are three parts to this method to make your recitation to be one of reflection and deep thought.

PART 1 – Pause at the end of each Ayah [verse]

To pause at the end of each Ayah is really important, because besides being a Sunnah of the Prophet ﷺ it is also a way for you to slow down in your recitation. Unfortunately, some people recite the Quran at 100 MPH; with such a recitation how can one gain Khushū'? Allah says:

$$وَرَتِّلِ الْقُرْآنَ تَرْتِيلًا$$

And recite the Quran in slow, measured rhythmic tones
(Quran [1] 73:4)

Umm Salamah ﷺ describes the recitation of the Prophet ﷺ as:

ذكرت أم سلمة رضي الله عنها قراءة رسول الله عليه وسلم (بسم الله الرحمن الرحيم ، وفي رواية : ثم يقف ثم يقول ، الحمد لله رب

العالمين ، الرحمن الرحيم ، وفي رواية : ثم يقف ثم يقول : ملك يوم
الدين) يقطّع قراءته آيةً آية

(بسم الله الرحمن الرحيم), and according to one report, he would pause, then say, (الحمد لله رب العالمين ، الرحمن) (الرحيم) Then according to one report, he would pause, then say, (ملك يوم الدين) and he would break up his recitation aayah by aayah. (Abu Dawood)

This is important, because if you don't pause, your recitation will not help you in understanding what you are reciting. Neither will it give you time to think about the meaning of the words in your recitation. Both of these are important because lacking these two ingredients will lead to a monotonous recitation. And if your Salah is a monotonous recitation then you will become bored with your recitation. I want you to enjoy the sweetness and joy of recitation of the Quran just as the pious predecessors did: you cannot achieve this with a 100 MPH recitation.

Note: Pausing at the end of each ayah is Sunnah even if the meaning continues into the next ayah.

PART 2 – Think about the Meaning of the words you are Reciting

Many people are unclear as to what we are supposed to think of as we are reciting the Quran in Salah, or praying behind an Imam and listening to him reciting.

The answer is to think about the meaning of what you are reciting. This of course requires you to learn Arabic, which is important for you to implement this step. Don't worry, we will look at the learning of Arabic in our fourth step of Action, where this will be covered in detail. But for now what you need to know is that you need to focus on the meaning of the passage that is being recited.

PART 3 – Ponder and Reflect over the response from Allah

Who are we that Allah should respond to us? Yet He does, because He loves us and He is Most Merciful to us. The Prophet ﷺ said:

When the servant says: (الحمد لله رب العالمين) (All praise is to Allah the Lord of the worlds), Allah says: 'My servant has praised Me.'

And when he says: (الرحمن الرحيم) (The Most Gracious The Most Merciful), Allah says: 'My servant has extolled Me,'

And when he says: (مالك يوم الدين) (Master of the Day of Judgement), Allah says: 'My servant has glorified Me' - and on one occasion He said: 'My servant has submitted to My power.'

And when he says: (إياك نعبد وإياك نستعين) (You alone we worship and from You alone we ask for help), He says: 'This is between Me and My servant, and My servant shall have what he has asked for.'

(You realise at this moment that throughout the day you may have worshipped your desires by pursuing them, you may have sinned, and you may have pursued your desires. This would bring tears to your eyes, because you would realise that you had not been true to this verse; because you chose instead to worship your desires by pursuing them. However, you then realise that your Lord is Forgiving and the Most Merciful. That is why most of the people of Khushū' would shake and tremble when they reached this verse. I have prayed behind many Imams who were unable to continue beyond this verse, they just broke down in tears because they felt they were not true in this verse.)

3

And when he says: (اهدنا الصراط المستقيم ، صراط الذين

أنعمت عليهم ، غير المغضوب عليهم ولا الضالين) (Show us the

straight path - The path of those on whom Thou hast
bestowed Thy Grace, - Those whose (portion) is not wrath
and who go not astray), He says: 'This is for My servant,
and My servant shall have what he has asked for.'"
(Muslim)

Allahu Akbar! Who are we to require a response from Allah? Do we
deserve a response from the King of all kings, the Lord of the
worlds? But because Allah is the Most Gracious, the Most Merciful,
Allah responds to us.

If someone says: I read the Quran but the Quran doesn't affect me,
then it is because until now he has not reflected and pondered
over the Quran.

You may say: 'Well, if I were to do this for the entire Quran, then it
will take me a very long time to go through all the Quranic
commentaries.' I am not saying that you must do this for the entire
Quran: but as a minimum make an honest attempt to do it for the
Surah that you recite everyday in your Salah (Surah Fatihah).
Merely by reflecting and pondering over this _one_ Surah, it will
make a huge difference to your level of Khushū', because Surah
Fatihah is the core of the Quran. The Prophet ﷺ called this Surah
(أُمُ القُرْان) The Essence of the Quran.

Which Category do You belong to?

People can be broadly grouped into four categories regarding their
interactions with the Quran:

The first category comprises those who are mainly concerned
about the standard of Tajweed of the Imam who is reciting. Did the
Imam prolong the letter according to the rules of Tajweed? Did he

pronounce the letter with a light sound, and so on? People in this category are mainly concerned about the rules of Tajweed.

The second category comprises those who are mainly concerned with the voice of the Imam. How beautiful was this Imam's voice? How soothing was his recitation? And so on.

The third category comprises those people who are concerned about the length of the Salah. They become agitated the moment the Imam exceeds a certain amount of time in the length of the Salah.

The fourth category comprises those who stop at every verse of the Quran, they ponder, and they reflect on every word and every verse during their recitation. If there is a command from Allah, then I want to submit myself to its obedience. If there is a prohibition, then I want to avoid doing it. If there is news, then I want to believe it. If there is a promise, then I want to make Du'a to Allah to allow me benefit from it. If there is a threat, then I seek refuge in Allah from it. This category of people comprises the ones who reflect deeply upon the Quran and ponder over every verse. The hearts of those who belong to this category are humbled in the remembrance of Allah.

أَلَمْ يَأْنِ لِلَّذِينَ آمَنُوا أَنْ تَخْشَعَ قُلُوبُهُمْ لِذِكْرِ اللَّهِ وَمَا نَزَلَ مِنَ الْحَقِّ

Has not the time arrived for the Believers that their hearts in all humility should engage in the remembrance of Allah. (Quran [1] 57:16)

This fourth category is the one you and I should be aiming for in our Salah.

2 – Crying during Recitation

The second necessesary component to experiencing the sweetness of recitation is crying when you recite the Quran. Most people find it difficult to cry when reciting the Quran: it is a common problem which cannot be ignored. I would like to ask you that if you are not going to cry when reciting the Quran, standing before the Almighty, the King of all kings, then when are you ever going to cry? If your heart does not soften when reciting the Quran, whilst reciting the best book on the face of this earth, error free, then when is your heart going to soften?

In the earlier part of this book, I explained in great detail the descriptions of the Prophet's crying ﷺ and his crying during his recitation of the Quran. In this section I want to share with you some of the tips that will make you cry during Salah.

Firstly, what is recommended is to cry, which is different from screaming or shouting. Crying is shedding tears. When the Prophet ﷺ entered Salah the sound of weeping 'like the sound of a boiling pot' could be heard coming from his chest, and this was due to his fear of Allah.

Abu Bakr ؓ upon entering Salah would cry whilst reciting. The Prophet ﷺ said to Aisha ؓ:

مُرِي أَبَا بَكْرٍ يُصَلِّي بِالنَّاسِ قَالَتْ إِنَّهُ رَجُلٌ أَسِيفٌ، مَتَى يَقُمْ مَقَامَكَ رَقَّ. فَعَادَ فَعَادَتْ، قَالَ شُعْبَةُ فَقَالَ فِي الثَّالِثَةِ أَوِ الرَّابِعَةِ: إِنَّكُنَّ صَوَاحِبُ يُوسُفَ، مُرُوا أَبَا بَكْرٍ

"Order Abu Bakr to lead the people in prayer." She replied, "Abu Bakr is a soft-hearted person and when he stands in your place, he will weep (so he will not be able to lead the prayer)." The Prophet ﷺ repeated the same order and she gave the same reply. The narrator, Shuba, said that the Prophet ﷺ said on the third or fourth time: "You are (like) the female companions of Joseph. Order Abu Bakr to lead the prayer." (Bukhari)

Abu Bakr ؓ would cry a lot, so the Prophet ﷺ said, he is the one who should lead the congregation. Because the Khushū' of the Imam will lead to the Khushū' of the congregation.

The tips that leads to Crying

The following tips and techniques will help you to cry whilst reciting the Quran. Not crying during recitation of the Quran is something to be concerned about. If you are not going to cry when reciting the Quran, then when are you going to cry?

If you follow the tips I am going to share with you here, not only will they help you to cry, but at the same time you will experience the sweetness of the recitation.

STEP 1 – Reading the Quran and pondering over its Meanings

We discussed this in detail earlier in this section.

STEP 2 – Knowing the virtues of Weeping

The Prophet ﷺ said:

لا يلج النار رجل بكى من خشية الله حتى يعود اللبن في الضرع

> A man who weeps for fear of Allah will not enter Hell until the milk goes back into the udder. (Tirmidhi)

"until the milk goes back into the udder" is a metaphor demonstrating that it is impossible for the one who weeps for the fear of Allah to enter into Hell.

The one who weeps for Allah will be under the shade of Allah, on that day when there will be no shade but His shade. The Prophet ﷺ mentioned seven people who will be under the shade of Allah, on that day when there will be no shade but His shade. Amongst them is a man who remembers Allah when he is alone and his eyes flow with tears. (Bukhari and Muslim)

STEP 3 – Reading the stories of how the Pious Predecessors Cried

The Salaf (the righteous predecessors) used to weep and grieve a great deal.

When Ata al-Sulaymi was asked: "What is this grief?" He said: "Woe to you! Death is close at hand, the grave is my house, on the Day of Resurrection I will stand and my path is over a bridge across Hell, and I do not know what will become of me."

Faddalah ibn Sayfi used to weep a great deal. A man entered upon him when he was weeping and said to his wife: "What is the matter with him?" She said: "He says that he wants to undertake a long journey and he does not have proper provision for it."

One night al-Hasan woke up weeping, and he disturbed the other people in the house with his weeping. They asked him what was the matter and he said: "I remembered a sin that I committed and I wept."

It was narrated that Tameem al-Daari ﷺ recited this verse (interpretation of the meaning): "Or do those who earn evil deeds think that We shall hold them equal with those who believe (in the Oneness of Allah-Tawheed) and do righteous good deeds," (Quran [3] 45:21) and he continued repeating it and weeping until morning came.

Hudhayfah ﷺ used to weep intensely, and it was said to him: "Why are you weeping?" He said: "I do not know what is ahead of me – Divine Pleasure or Divine Wrath."

STEP 4 – Listening to moving Speeches and Lectures

It was narrated that al-Irbad ibn Sariyah ﷺ, who was one of those who used to weep, said: "The Messenger of Allah delivered a deeply moving speech at which our eyes began to overflow and our hearts melted." (Tirmidhi, Abu Dawood)
(islamqa.info)

These tips and suggestions will help you to weep before the Almighty Allah. If you still find it difficult to cry, then pretend to be crying. The Prophet ﷺ said:

اقْرَءُوا الْقُرْآنَ وَابْكُوا فَإِنْ لَمْ تَجِدُوا بُكَاءً فَتَبَاكَوْا

Recite the Quran and cry. If you cannot cry, then pretend to cry. (Ibn Majah)

Follow these tips on how to weep before Allah, and put them into practice. If you weep whilst reciting the Quran and you ponder and reflect during your recitation, then you will enjoy this experience so much that you may not even realize that you have recited the whole of Surah Baqarah without a trace of tiredness or inattention.

3

P A R A D I S E

A is for . . . Arabic

Allah tells us in the Quran that this book is a book of guidance:

شَهْرُ رَمَضَانَ الَّذِي أُنْزِلَ فِيهِ الْقُرْآنُ هُدًى لِلنَّاسِ

Ramadan is the (month) in which was sent down the Quran as a guide to mankind. (Quran [1] 2:185a)

This means that the Quran is not merely a book of recitation or a just a means to earn rewards. Yes, you will be rewarded for reciting the Quran: 10 rewards for every letter, as has been said by the Prophet ﷺ. However, the main purpose of its revelation was for it to be a source of guidance for us all.

So: the Quran is a book of guidance. You can only be guided by it if you understand it so that you may then implement it. If you don't understand it then how can you benefit from its guidance? Suppose you recite the following verses of the Quran in your Salah:

يَا أَيُّهَا الَّذِينَ آمَنُوا إِنَّمَا الْخَمْرُ وَالْمَيْسِرُ وَالْأَنْصَابُ وَالْأَزْلَامُ رِجْسٌ مِنْ عَمَلِ الشَّيْطَانِ فَاجْتَنِبُوهُ لَعَلَّكُمْ تُفْلِحُونَ

O ye who believe! Intoxicants and gambling, (dedication of) stones, and (divination by) arrows, are an abomination— of Satan's handiwork: eschew [abstain from] such (abomination), that ye may prosper. (Quran [1] 5:90)

How will you abstain from these evil acts, if you don't know Arabic?

Suppose your close friend sends you a letter in a language that you don't understand, wouldn't you get a translator to translate your friend's letter for you? At the very least, you would use a dictionary or something in order to understand this letter, wouldn't you? Then how about the Quran, the message from Your Creator, Allah, and understanding His message? Without understanding the Quran, your recitation is a recitation without a spirit or a soul.

This means that you cannot benefit from the guidance of the Quran without understanding it, and if you do not work towards that understanding, your recitation may not prevent you from evil and sins, which is the main purpose of Salah.

إِنَّ الصَّلَاةَ تَنْهَىٰ عَنِ الْفَحْشَاءِ وَالْمُنْكَرِ

For Prayer restrains from shameful and unjust deeds
(Quran [1] 29:45)

Secondly, if you do not know Arabic as a language, then you cannot expect to have Khushū' in your Salah because you do not understand what you are asking for from Allah. The most important ingredient for an accepted Salah is having sincerity. If you do not know what you are asking for from Allah, how can you truly be sincere?

Therefore, if you do not know Arabic, you are losing out on two things which are preventing you from developing Khushū' in your Salah:

1. Lack of guidance from the Quran;
2. Lack of sincerity.

In order to increase your level of guidance from the Quran and the level of sincerity, you need to understand Arabic.

Is translation sufficient?

Translation helps to a certain extent, but there are two main obstacles preventing any translation from being complete or accurate.

Firstly, when Allah links two things together in the Quran, they cannot be taken apart. Allah says in the Quran:

$$\text{وَالْقُرْآنِ الْحَكِيمِ}$$

By the Quran, full of Wisdom (Quran [1] 36:2)

Allah has called the Quran a book of wisdom. The book of wisdom and the Quran go hand in hand: they cannot be separated. If I were to ask: 'What is the book of wisdom?' The answer would be, 'The Quran'. If I were to ask: 'What is the Quran?' The answer would be, 'The Book of Wisdom'. So when Allah puts two things together in the Quran, they cannot be separated.

Similarly, Allah has linked Quran with the Arabic language. Allah says:

$$\text{إِنَّا أَنْزَلْنَاهُ قُرْآنًا عَرَبِيًّا لَعَلَّكُمْ تَعْقِلُونَ}$$

We have sent it down, as an Arabic Quran, so that you may understand. (Quran [2] 12:2)

Allah has linked the Quran with Arabic and understanding it. So Allah requires you to understand the language.

Secondly, when you translate something into another language, you lose many of the subtle qualities of the original. Consider: does the translation of a work of Shakespeare into German or Arabic have the same beauty as the original? The answer would be no, because when you translate anything, the beauty of the original is lost.

Similarly, if you were to read the translation of the Quran, yes you may get the gist of the overall message but you have lost the beauty that is in the Quran. Though the translation may be beautiful itself, that beauty is not the same as the beauty of the original.

Can you learn Arabic in 24 Hours?

I am assuming that you may well be asking yourself at this point, whether in order to develop Khushū', you need to spend 4-5 years learning Arabic as a language? And if you don't spend the time learning this language, does that mean that you will never be able to achieve Khushū'?

Yes, you need to learn Arabic, but it is a misconception that learning it will take you a long time. Of course, there is no limit to knowledge: the further you go into the ocean, the deeper you realize it is. But if you want to learn Arabic so that you are able to develop Khushū' in your Salah, then it will not take you as long as you might think. If you get hold of my book 'Master Quranic Arabic in 24 Hours', this book focuses on two main things:

1. All the words are directly taken from the Quran, so your time will not be wasted in learning words that you may never use.
2. Each lesson is 1 hour long, and there are 24, 1-hour lessons. Which means that if you do 1 hour per day, in 24 days you will have a good enough level of Arabic to be able to develop Khushū' in your Salah.

4

This step is vital. If you follow my recommendations, your recitation of the Quran in your Salah will become a source of guidance for you. Also, you will feel more sincere standing before Allah because you will be understanding what you are asking from Him in your Salah. I want you to experience both of these benefits in your Salah: therefore learn Arabic, and never let Shaitan whisper to you that you will do it later or that this is not for you. Any whisper that prevents you from developing Khushū' is from Shaitan and Allah tells us in the Quran that 'Satan is an enemy to you: so treat him as an enemy' (Qur'an [1] 35:6).

P A R A D I S E

D is for . . . Du'a

The place of Khushū' lies in the heart and since it lies in the heart, the issue of Khushū' is referred to Allah, because Allah is the changer of hearts, and no one can rectify a heart other than Allah.

In order to change your heart you need the help of Allah. Allah's help is so important that if you don't have His help, no matter how many tips and techniques I share with you in this book, they will not help you. Allah says in the Quran:

$$إِنْ يَنْصُرْكُمُ اللَّهُ فَلَا غَالِبَ لَكُمْ ۖ وَإِنْ يَخْذُلْكُمْ فَمَنْ ذَا الَّذِي يَنْصُرُكُمْ مِنْ بَعْدِهِ ۗ وَعَلَى اللَّهِ فَلْيَتَوَكَّلِ الْمُؤْمِنُون$$

> If Allah helps you, none can overcome you: if He forsakes you, who is there after that that can help you? In Allah, then, let believers put their trust. (Quran [1] 3:160)

Ask Allah to give you a heart full of humility and submissiveness. The Prophet ﷺ would make Du'a to Allah and say the following:

$$اَللَّهُمَّ إِنِّي أَعُوذُ بِكَ مِنْ قَلْبٍ لاَ يَخْشَعُ، وَمِنْ دُعَاءٍ لاَ يُسْمَعُ، وَمِنْ نَفْسٍ لاَ تَشْبَعُ، وَمِنْ عِلْمٍ لاَ يَنْفَعُ$$

> "O Allah, I seek refuge with you from a heart that does not possess khushū', from supplications which are not accepted, from the evil desire which is never satisfied and from any non-beneficial knowledge." (Tirmidhi, Abu Dawood)

This step of making Du'a is so important that if you make Du'a to Allah to grant you Khushū', then without any doubt Allah will give you Khushū' and number you amongst the people of Khushū'. Allah says:

وَقَالَ رَبُّكُمُ ادْعُونِي أَسْتَجِبْ لَكُمْ

And your Lord says: "Call on Me; I will answer your (Prayer) (Quran [1] 40:60)

On the other hand, when you don't make Du'a to Allah, and you don't ask Allah for something that you want, then Allah becomes angry. If He is angry with you, how can you expect Allah to grant you Khushū' in your Salah?

من لم يسأل الله يغضب عليه

If one does not ask Allah, He will get angry with him (Tirmidhi)

The more concerned you are about Khushū', the more you will make Du'a to Allah. The majority of people make the most Du'a for the things that they are mainly concerned about. Therefore, have concern for developing Khushū' in your Salah because the development of Khushū is related to your Hereafter, so make anything related to the Hereafter your greatest concern. The Prophet ﷺ would make Du'a to Allah and say:

5

اللهم لا تجعل الدنيا أكبر همنا ولا مبلغ علمنا

O Allah don't make this world our biggest concern (Tirmidhi)

When the Hereafter becomes your greatest concern, this will increase your Du'a to Allah for granting you Khushū'.

1 – Start With Du'a

The Prophet ﷺ would make the following Du'a to Allah upon starting his Salah:

اللَّهُمَّ بَاعِدْ بَيْنِي وَبَيْنَ خَطَايَاىَ كَمَا بَاعَدْتَ بَيْنَ الْمَشْرِقِ وَالْمَغْرِبِ،

اللَّهُمَّ نَقِّنِي مِنَ الْخَطَايَا كَمَا يُنَقَّى الثَّوْبُ الْأَبْيَضُ مِنَ الدَّنَسِ، اللَّهُمَّ اغْسِلْ خَطَايَاىَ بِالْمَاءِ وَالثَّلْجِ وَالْبَرَدِ

O Allah! Set me apart from my sins (faults) as the East and West are set apart from each other and clean me from faults as a white garment is cleaned of dirt (after thorough washing). O Allah! Wash off my sins with water, snow and hail. (Bukhari)

From your next Salah, start to build a habit in making this same Du'a that was made by the Prophet ﷺ.

2 – End with Du'a

Pride and arrogance are dangerous. If you feel that your Salah is better than your neighbour's Salah, that your Salah has Khushū' greater than his, and so you look down upon the Salah of others and you feel pride in your Salah, *this will destroy your Khushū'*. Allah does not like pride and arrogance. Therefore, in order to avoid pride and arrogance creeping into your heart, there is one more action you must take.

When you finish your Salah, immediately humble yourself as much as you can, and turn to Allah and say, 'O My Lord, I didn't humble myself the way I should have, I didn't stand before you the way I should have, O My Lord forgive me.' Confess and be remorseful towards Allah for your shortcomings in the Salah. Never assume perfection in your Salah.

Remind yourself of the blessings of Allah, and say 'O My Lord, Your right is the greatest, O, You Who gave life to me whilst I was nothing, O, You Who fed me whilst I was hungry, O, You Who clothed me whilst I was without clothing, O, You Who gave me knowledge whilst I was ignorant, O, You Who guided me whilst I was misguided, O, You Who pointed me to this prostration, O, You Who gave me health and well-being, O My Lord these are your blessings and this is my shortcoming; I confess to you that I never stood before you like the standing of the people of Khushū', O My Lord, I confess to You my weakness and my scarcity of substance.' Humble yourself before Allah using such Du'a's and have full trust in Allah because He is the Most Merciful. By doing this you will leave the place of Salah with your faults amended, your reward increased, and your status raised.

Never assume that your Salah is better than another's. Many people were given Khushū' but it was taken away from them. Many people did not have Khushū' but, after humbling themselves and asking Allah to amend their faults, they were granted Khushū'.

Dear reader, you are dealing with the Most Merciful. Humble yourself immediately after the Salah, and ask Allah in all humility to amend the shortcomings in your Salah. Your Salah can never be of sufficient worth to befit His Majesty and His Greatness. It is by the mercy of Allah that He accepts your Salah even with all the shortcomings and faults that it contains.

Ibn Qayyim (رحمة الله عليه) gives an amazing example illustrating this point. He says, suppose that you are invited by the king with a group of people, and everyone is bringing a present for the king. One is bringing a diamond, another is bringing some gold and everyone is bringing expensive items. But you cannot afford to give this king anything expensive, therefore, you take a loaf of bread. Do you think that the king will accept your loaf of bread?

5

This is how we present our Salah before the Almighty: we imagine that it is worthy of acceptance and become proud, whereas our Salah is like that loaf of bread, which has no value compared to the greatness of Allah or the offerings of others. It is by the mercy of Allah that He accepts our Salah with all its shortcomings and faults. But Allah is the One who amends all faults and accepts it out of His Mercy.

This reflection and Du'a to Allah after your Salah will remove this disease of pride and arrogance in your Salah.

3 – Du'a during Sajdah

When you are in Sajdah, do not raise your head up in haste. Prolong your Sajdah: this is a sign of Khushū'. Doing Sajdah in haste is a sign of pride and arrogance. Iblees didn't perform Sajdah to Adam ﷺ because of his pride and arrogance.

Prolong in your Sajdah, because that is the time when you are the nearest to your Lord.

أَقْرَبُ مَا يَكُونُ الْعَبْدُ مِنْ رَبِّهِ وَهُوَ سَاجِدٌ فَأَكْثِرُوا الدُّعَاءَ

The nearest a servant comes to his Lord is when he is prostrating himself, so make supplication (in this state). (Muslim)

Therefore, make Du'a to Allah as much as you can but do not recite the Quran in the Sajdah. The Prophet ﷺ said:

إِنِّي نُهِيتُ أَنْ أَقْرَأَ الْقُرْآنَ رَاكِعًا أَوْ سَاجِدًا فَأَمَّا الرُّكُوعُ فَعَظِّمُوا فِيهِ الرَّبَّ عَزَّ وَجَلَّ وَأَمَّا السُّجُودُ فَاجْتَهِدُوا فِي الدُّعَاءِ فَقَمِنٌ أَنْ يُسْتَجَابَ لَكُمْ

Indeed I have been forbidden to recite the Quran in the positions of bowing and prostration. So far as Ruk'u is concerned, extol in it the Great and Glorious Lord, and while prostrating yourselves be earnest in supplication, for it is fitting that your supplications should be answered. (Muslim)

Aisha ﷺ reported that the Messenger of Allah ﷺ used to pronounce while bowing and prostrating himself:

سُبُّوحٌ قُدُّوسٌ رَبُّ الْمَلَائِكَةِ وَالرُّوح

All Glorious, All Holy, Lord of the Angels and the Spirit. (Muslim)

Aisha ﷺ narrates:

One night I missed Allah's Messenger ﷺ from the bed, and when I sought him my hand touched the soles of his feet while he was in prostration; they (feet) were raised and he was saying:

اللَّهُمَّ أَعُوذُ بِرِضَاكَ مِنْ سَخَطِكَ وَبِمُعَافَاتِكَ مِنْ عُقُوبَتِكَ وَأَعُوذُ بِكَ مِنْكَ لاَ أُحْصِي ثَنَاءً عَلَيْكَ أَنْتَ كَمَا أَثْنَيْتَ عَلَى نَفْسِكَ

"O Allah, I seek refuge in Your pleasure from Your anger, and in Your forgiveness from Your punishment, and I seek refuge in You from You (Your anger). I cannot reckon Your praise. You are as You have lauded Yourself." (Muslim)

Memorise these Du'as of the Prophet ﷺ, prolong your Sajdah without raising your head up too hastily, be engaged in Du'a, for it is fitting that your supplications should be answered.

Du'as of the Prophet ﷺ during Sajdah

(1)

It was narrated from Abdullah bin Masood ﷺ that the Prophet ﷺ used to say when prostrating:

سَجَدَ لَكَ سَوَادِي وَخَيَالِي، وَآمَنَ بِكَ فُؤَادِي، أَبُوءُ بِنِعْمَتِكَ عَلَيَّ، هَذِهِ يَدَايَ وَمَا جَنَيْتُ عَلَى نَفْسِي

My body and my shadow have prostrated to You; my heart has believed in You; I acknowledge Your favours towards me: here are my hands and whatever I have earned against myself.

(Bazzar)

(2)

It was narrated from Jabir bin 'Abdullah ﷺ that the Prophet ﷺ used to say when prostrating:

اللَّهُمَّ لَكَ سَجَدْتُ وَبِكَ آمَنْتُ ، وَلَكَ أَسْلَمْتُ، سَجَدَ وَجْهِي لِلَّذِي خَلَقَهُ وَصَوَّرَهُ وَشَقَّ سَمْعَهُ وَبَصَرَهُ، تَبَارَكَ اللهُ أَحْسَنُ الْخَالِقِينَ

O Allah, unto You I have prostrated and in You I have believed, and unto You I have submitted. My face has prostrated before He Who created it and fashioned it, and brought forth its faculties of hearing and seeing. Blessed is Allah, the Best of creators.

(Muslim)

(3)

Abu Hurairah ﷺ reported: The Messenger of Allah ﷺ used to say in his prostration:

اللَّهُمَّ اغْفِرْ لِي ذَنْبِي كُلَّهُ ، دِقَّهُ وَجِلَّهُ ، وَأَوَّلَهُ وَآخِرَهُ ، وَعَلَانِيَتَهُ وَسِرَّهُ

O Allah, forgive me all of my sins, the small and great of them, the first and last of them, and the seen and hidden of them.

(Muslim)

(4)

Aisha ﷺ reported: One night I missed Allah's Messenger ﷺ from the bed, and when I sought him my hand touched the soles of his feet while he was in the state of prostration; they (feet) were raised and he was saying:

اللَّهُمَّ إِنِّي أَعُوذُ بِرِضَاكَ مِنْ سَخَطِكَ ، وَبِمُعَافَاتِكَ مِنْ عُقُوبَتِكَ ، وَأَعُوذُ

بِكَ مِنْكَ ، لَا أُحْصِي ثَنَاءً عَلَيْكَ أَنْتَ كَمَا أَثْنَيْتَ عَلَى نَفْسِكَ

O Allah, I seek refuge with Your pleasure from Your anger and with Your pardon from Your punishment, and I seek refuge with You from You. I cannot enumerate Your praise, You are as You have praised Yourself.

(Muslim)

(5)

It was narrated that Ibn Abbas ؓ said: The Prophet ﷺ when he prostrated he said:

اللَّهُمَّ اجْعَلْ فِي قَلْبِي نُورًا وَاجْعَلْ فِي سَمْعِي نُورًا وَاجْعَلْ فِي بَصَرِي نُورًا وَاجْعَلْ مِنْ تَحْتِي نُورًا وَاجْعَلْ مِنْ فَوْقِي نُورًا وَعَنْ يَمِينِي نُورًا وَعَنْ يَسَارِي نُورًا وَاجْعَلْ أَمَامِي نُورًا وَاجْعَلْ خَلْفِي نُورًا وَأَعْظِمْ لِي نُورًا

O Allah, place light in my heart, and place light in my hearing, and place light in my seeing, and place light beneath me, and place light above me, and light on my right, and light on my left, and place light behind me, and make the light greater for me.

(Nasai)

Du'as of the Prophet ﷺ during Ruku'

(1)

Ali b. Abu Talib ؓ reported that when the Messenger of Allah ﷺ would bow, he would say:

اللَّهُمَّ لَكَ رَكَعْتُ وَبِكَ آمَنْتُ ، وَلَكَ أَسْلَمْتُ خَشَعَ لَكَ سَمْعِي ، وَبَصَرِي ، وَمُخِّي ، وَعَظْمِي ، وَعَصَبِي

O Allah, unto You I have bowed, and in You I have believed, and to You I have submitted. My hearing, and

147

my sight, and my mind, and my bones, and my tendons, are humbled before you.

(Muslim)

(2)

It was narrated from Muhammad bin Maslamah ﷺ that: When the Messenger of Allah ﷺ stood to offer a voluntary prayer, he would say when he bowed:

اللَّهُمَّ لَكَ رَكَعْتُ وَبِكَ آمَنْتُ وَلَكَ أَسْلَمْتُ وَعَلَيْكَ تَوَكَّلْتُ أَنْتَ رَبِّي خَشَعَ سَمْعِي وَبَصَرِي وَلَحْمِي وَدَمِي وَمُخِّي وَعَصَبِي لِلَّهِ رَبِّ الْعَالَمِينَ

O Allah, to You I have bowed, in You I believe, to You I have submitted and in You I put my trust. You are my Lord. My hearing, my sight, my flesh, my blood, my brain and my tendons are humbled before Allah, the Lord of the Worlds.

(Nasai)

Du'as of the Prophet ﷺ during Sajdah and Ruku'

(1)

It was narrated that Hudhaifah ﷺ said "I prayed with the Messenger of Allah ﷺ, and he bowed and said when bowing:

سُبْحَانَ رَبِّيَ الْعَظِيمِ

Glory be to my Lord Almighty.

And when prostrating:

سُبْحَانَ رَبِّيَ الأَعْلَى

Glory be to my Lord Most High

(Nasai)

(2)

Aisha ﷺ reported: that the Prophet ﷺ used to say in his bowings and prostrations:

سُبْحَانَكَ اللَّهُمَّ رَبَّنَا وَبِحَمْدِكَ اللَّهُمَّ اغْفِرْ لِي

How far from imperfections You are O Allah, our Lord, and I praise You. O Allah, forgive me.
(Bukhari and Muslim)

(3)

Aisha ﷺ reported: that the Prophet ﷺ used to say in his bowings and prostrations:

سُبُّوحٌ قُدُّوسٌ رَبُّ الْمَلَائِكَةِ وَالرُّوحِ

Perfect and Holy (He is), Lord of the angels and the Rooh (i.e. Jibraeel).

(Muslim)

(4)

Awf bin Malik ﷺ said: "I prayed Qiyam with the Prophet ﷺ. He stood and started reciting Al-Baqarah and he did not come to any verse that spoke of mercy but he paused and asked for mercy, and he did not come to any verse that spoke of punishment but he paused (and sought refuge with Allah from that). Then he bowed and he stayed bowing for as long as he had stood, and he said while bowing:

سُبْحَانَ ذِي الْجَبَرُوتِ ، والْمَلَكُوتِ ، والْكِبْرِيَاءِ ، وَالْعَظَمَةِ

How far from imperfections He is, The Possessor of total power, sovereignty, magnificence and grandeur.

Then he prostrated for as long as he had bowed, saying while prostrating:

سُبْحَانَ ذِي الْجَبَرُوتِ ، والْمَلَكُوتِ ، والْكِبْرِيَاءِ ، وَالْعَظَمَةِ

How far from imperfections He is, The Possessor of total
power, sovereignty, magnificence and grandeur.

Then he recited Al Imran, then another surah and another, doing
that each time."

(Nasai)

Memorise these Du'as of the Prophet ﷺ, prolong your Sajdah
without raising your head up too hastily, be engaged in Du'a, for it
is fitting that your supplications should be answered.

PARAD■SE

I is for . . . Imagination

Picture a scene in which you are working in a company, and your company wants you to relocate to another country for a few years. As you prepare to leave this country, imagine this is going to be your last time with your loved ones. What would your state of mind be? Would your feelings when meeting them on this last day be the same as that when meeting them every day?

I am assuming that your state would be different on both occasions. You would be more sad, maybe even shedding tears on this last day because this could be your last time of seeing your loved ones and you will be unsure of when you will see them again.

hen you stand in Salah, never take it for granted that you will be getting another opportunity to stand for your next Salah. This step of imagining your Salah to be the last one in your life is very important, because if you don't do this, then you might not cry as much, you might not prolong your Sajdah. In imagining that this Salah might be your last, you probably won't be distracted.

Imagine for every Salah that you pray that it is your last Salah; that after this Salah you will die and you will leave this world.

جَاءَ رَجُلٌ إِلَى النَّبِيِّ صلى الله عليه وسلم فَقَالَ يَا رَسُولَ اللَّهِ عَلِّمْنِي
وَأَوْجِزْ قَالَ إِذَا قُمْتَ فِي صَلَاتِكَ فَصَلِّ صَلَاةَ مُوَدِّعٍ وَلَا تَكَلَّمْ بِكَلَامٍ
تَعْتَذِرُ مِنْهُ وَأَجْمِعِ الْيَأْسَ عَمَّا فِي أَيْدِي النَّاسِ "

A man came to the Prophet ﷺ and said: 'O Messenger of Allah, teach me but make it concise.' He said: 'When you stand to pray, pray like a man bidding farewell. Do not say anything for which you will have to apologize. And give up hope for what other people have.' (Ibn Majah)

6

Ask yourself: if you prayed your next Salah as though it were your last one, would you pray this Salah with distractions in your mind? Would you pray this Salah in a hasty manner? Would you pray this Salah planning what you were going to do afterwards?

There is no guarantee that you will get the opportunity for your next Salah. In fact there is no guarantee that you will finish the Salah that you are praying. How many righteous servants of Allah have left this world whilst in Sajdah? How many righteous servants of Allah have left this world before completing their Salah?

Shaykh Abdul Hameed Kashak, one Friday, had a bath, got dressed in white clothes, and perfumed himself. After which, whilst praying the second Rak'ah of the Sunnah of Wudhu, he fell. His family all gathered to see what had happened, and they found that his soul had returned to Allah.

Amir Ibn Abdullah Zubair was on his death-bed in his last throes. His family were around him weeping. Upon hearing the call to prayer for Maghrib Salah, he said to the people around him, 'Hold my hands and take me.' 'Where?' they asked, upon which he replied, 'To the Masjid.' 'And whilst you are in this situation?' 'Allah be Glorified, I am listening to the caller of the prayer and I do not respond? Hold my hands and take me to the Masjid.' They picked him up and took him to the Masjid, he offered one Rak'ah with the Imam and then died in Sajdah.

There are many stories of the righteous servants of Allah who spent the last moments of their life in Sajdah: this shows us that there is no guarantee that you will finish the Salah that you are praying, leave aside a guarantee of praying your next Salah.

Pray every Salah as if it were your last. If you are about to pray Maghrib Salah, imagine that this is your last Salah of your life and that you will never get an opportunity to pray another Salah after this one. Imagine that after this Salah, you will be returning to Allah, and either you will be amongst the successful ones or amongst the losers. This will make you fear losing the rewards of this Salah so you turn to Allah with humility and with full hearted submissiveness and pray this Salah like a man bidding farewell to the world.

Imagine a person who has been told that so and so person is going to kill him in the next 10 minutes. So he says, 'Give me some time between me and my Lord so I can pray.' How much Khushū' would this person have during his Salah knowing he will be killed after 10 minutes?

How many people now living are unaware that their graves are already dug?

A woman from the Tribe of Israel fasted for over forty years. She was asked how she fasted for such a long period, upon which she replied: 'Every morning I would say to myself that this was the last day of my life, this would encourage me to fast, and so I fasted. I have the desire to end my life whilst fasting.' This ability to imagine led her to fast for over forty years.

This was of course in the previous Shari'ah, in the present Shari'ah it is not allowed to fast continuously in this way. The point that I am illustrating here is to show how people have been guided in their Khushū' by their imagination of their deeds as their last deed, hoping for Allah's mercy and fearing His punishment.

6

P A R A D I S E

S is for . . . Stance

Imagine that you are being invited by the king to spend some time with him in his palace. Upon accepting his invitation when you arrive at his palace, how would you stand before him? Would you ever stand before him in a disrespectful manner? I am sure that you would stand with respect. If you wouldn't stand before this king in a disrespectful manner, then how about the King of all kings? How about the Lord of the worlds? How about the One Who created you? How about the One Who showers blessings day and night upon you even while you sleep? How about the One Who loves you more than your own mother loves you? How can you stand disrespectfully before Allah?

There is no better way of standing respectfully than the way of the Prophet ﷺ. His way of standing before Allah is the way which you and I should be imitating. Imitate the way he stood, because there is no better way than his way. The Prophet ﷺ said:

صلوا كما رأيتموني أصلي

Pray as you have seen me praying. (Bukhari)

If you grasp this point of stance then it can make a real difference in your Salah. This posture will give you confidence because it is the best stance for developing Khushū'. On the other hand, if you don't follow the Prophet's ﷺ example, you will be doubtful all the time as to the correct way to stand. This may lead to you trying various positions, trying to get it right, but no matter how much you try, if your stance is different to that of the Prophet ﷺ it will not work.

I am going to divide this section into two parts to make the correct stance crystal clear and simple. I will also tell you the things that you must NOT do during your standing.

154

1 – Correct Stance for the Development of Khushū'

This is the stance that you must adopt during your Salah. There are four components in order to develop a stance conducive to Khushū'. I will go through each component with you and show you the way to get to a stance that is conducive to the development of Khushū'.

1. Facing the Direction of the Qiblah

Standing facing the Qiblah at the time of Salah is a command given by Allah to the Muslims. This brings unity amongst the Muslims when praying. Allah says:

وَمِنْ حَيْثُ خَرَجْتَ فَوَلِّ وَجْهَكَ شَطْرَ الْمَسْجِدِ الْحَرَامِ وَحَيْثُ مَا كُنْتُمْ فَوَلُّوا وُجُوهَكُمْ شَطْرَهُ

> Now, turn your face in the direction of the Sacred Mosque (Al-Masjid-ul-Haram), and (O Muslims), wherever you are, turn your faces in its direction. (Quran [2] 2: 144)

Facing the Qiblah whilst praying is one of the pillars of Salah, without which Salah is not valid. There are certain exceptions: it does not apply to those who are unable to do it, such as one who is sick, or one who is traveling in a car or on a plane, etc.

2. Raising the Hands – how it is to be done

You should raise the hands when saying the Takbir to the level of your shoulders, or alternatively, to the level of your earlobes; both are reported of Prophet ﷺ

كان رسول الله صلى الله عليه وسلم إذا افتتح الصلاة رفع يديه حتى يحاذي منكبيه

> The Prophet ﷺ would raise his hands opposite the shoulders at the time of beginning the prayer. (Muslim)

7

كَانَ رسول الله صلى الله عليه وسلم إِذَا كَبَّرَ رَفَعَ يَدَيْهِ حَتَّى يُحَاذِيَ
بِهِمَا أُذُنَيْهِ

The Prophet ﷺ would raise his hands opposite his ears at the time of reciting the takbeer. (Muslim)

The wisdom behind raising your hands at the beginning of Salah was discussed earlier in the 'Preparation' step for developing Khushū'.

3. Posture of Absolute Devotion

Placing the right hand over the left hand is a Sunnah of the Prophet ﷺ. Wail Ibn Hajr ؓ whilst describing the prayer of the Prophet ﷺ said:

وضع يده اليمنى على اليسرى

The Prophet ﷺ placed his right hand on his left. (Muslim)

This placing of the hands and the standing position shows the posture of someone who is humble and it is a stance of veneration. This is why such a posture is disliked by the scholars for anyone other than Allah. A stance in which there is such veneration is only befitting to Allah. Allah says in the Quran:

وَقُومُوا لِلَّهِ قَانِتِينَ

And stand before Allah in total devotion. (Quran [2] 2:238)

4. Protecting Your Eyes From Wandering

Imagine that you are driving your car on the motorway: I would expect your eyes to be focused on the road. If your eyes weren't focused on the road but were wandering, what do you think would happen? You will be distracted from your driving and possibly may cause a serious accident.

This is exactly the result of your Salah if you don't protect your eyes from wandering. When your eyes are wandering, it will cause distractions in your Salah, and distractions will destroy your Khushū'.

Therefore, where do you train to keep your eyes? There is no one better to tell us where to fix the gaze during Salah than the Prophet ﷺ.

Aisha ؓ narrates:

دخل رسول الله صلى الله عليه وسلم الكعبة ما خلف بصره موضع سجوده حتى خرج منها

When the Prophet ﷺ entered the Ka'abah, his eyes never left the place of his prostration until he came out again. (Hakim).

Further Aisha ؓ narrates:

كان رسول الله صلى الله عليه و سلم إذا صلى طأطأ رأسه و رمى ببصره نحو الأرض

The Prophet ﷺ used to pray with his head tilted forward and his gaze lowered, looking at the ground. (Hakim).

Therefore, throughout your Salah, your eyes must be fixed on the place of your prostration and by doing this, you will save your eyes from wandering during Salah, which can cause distractions that could result in your Khushū' being ruined.

On the other hand, if you fix your gaze on the place of prostration, you will be rewarded by Allah for following the way of the Prophet ﷺ.

7

Secondly, training your eyes on the place of prostration means less probability of distraction in your Salah, which is what you need.

At the Time of Tashahhud

When you sit for Tashahhud, look at the finger with which you are pointing, as it was reported that the Prophet ﷺ:

يشير بأصبعه التي تلي الإبهام إلى القبلة ويرمي ببصره إليها

"Would point with the finger next to the thumb towards the Qiblah, and focus his gaze upon it." (Ibn Khuzaymah)

According to another narration, he

"Pointed with his index finger and did not allow his gaze to wander beyond it." (Ahmad and Abu Dawood)

2 – Doubtful Creator Stance

There is a stance which I call a 'Doubtful Creator Stance', because what I am going to share with you here are some of the things that some people do in order to develop Khushū' in their Salah but unfortunately instead of Khushū' being developed, it is reduced from their Salah. It is really important for these to be highlighted because unfortunately, these are quite common, and people actually believe that doing these things will bring about Khushū' in their Salah. So they implement these things, but it does not develop Khushū', and their posture becomes doubtful because it lacks confidence. They keep on trying different ways to develop Khushū' yet they are still in doubt.

Closing the Eyes to encourage Khushū'

One behaviour that is commonly used is the closing of the eyes during Salah to help develop Khushū'.

Hadiths have already been mentioned earlier telling us that the Prophet ﷺ would look at the place of prostration during his Salah.

The scholars are agreed that it is disliked 'to close the eyes for no reason when praying.' (al-Rawd al-Murabba', 1/95) (Manaar al-Sabeel, 1/66; al-Kaafi, 1/285).

If you were to ask those who close their eyes during Salah whether or not it helps them with Khushū', most of them would respond that their Salah still lacks Khushū'. We know that there is no one more eager to experience Khushū' than the Prophet ﷺ, so if he never did this in his Salah, then who are we to come up with this amazing idea?

Therefore, by closing your eyes you are, firstly, not following the Sunnah of the Prophet ﷺ and secondly, it is a false belief that closing your eyes will help you achieve Khushū'.

On the other hand, if you have your eyes on the place of prostration, then you will be following the Sunnah of the Prophet ﷺ and you will be on the right path for developing Khushū'.

> Note: Ibn Qayyim (رحمة الله عليه) writes regarding this matter and says: "The correct view is that if keeping the eyes open does not affect a person's khushū', then this is better, but if keeping the eyes open affects a person's khushū' because of decorations, ornaments, etc. in front of him, which distract him, then it is not makrūh at all for him to close his eyes. The opinion that indeed it is mustahab in this case is closer to the principles and aims of Shari'ah than holding it to be makrūh. And Allah knows best." (Zaad al-Ma'ād)

Thus it is clear that the Sunnah is not to close one's eyes, unless it is necessary to do so in order to avoid something that may adversely affect one's Khushū'. Allah knows best.

Gazing upwards during Salah

Gazing upwards loses concentration in Salah. The Prophet ﷺ

forbade us looking towards the sky during Salah, he said:

" مَا بَالُ أَقْوَامٍ يَرْفَعُونَ أَبْصَارَهُمْ إِلَى السَّمَاءِ فِي صَلَاتِهِمْ ". فَاشْتَدَّ
قَوْلُهُ فِي ذَلِكَ حَتَّى قَالَ " لَيَنْتَهُنَّ عَنْ ذَلِكَ أَوْ لَتُخْطَفَنَّ أَبْصَارُهُمْ "

What is wrong with those people who look towards the sky during the prayer?" His talk grew stern while delivering this speech and he said, "They should stop (looking towards the sky during the prayer); otherwise their eyesight would be taken away." (Bukhari)

The only place where your eyes should be focused for a stance conducive to Khushū' is the way of the Prophet ﷺ, which is by looking at your place of prostration.

Humbling your body without humbling your heart – Khushū' of Hypocrisy

Khushu is developed in the heart and the results of it manifest on the body. This brings to mind the hadith of the Prophet ﷺ who said: "Beware! There is a piece of flesh in the body, if it becomes good (reformed), the whole body becomes good, but if it gets spoilt, the whole body gets spoilt and that is the heart." (Bukhari)

Your heart is the centre of Khushū'.

Umar ؓ saw a man lowering his neck in the prayer, so he said to him: "O companion of the (bent) neck! Raise your neck. Khushū' is not in (lowering) the neck, rather Khushū' is in the heart." (Madarij Salikeen)

When you have Khushū' in your heart, your physical body humbles itself.

You may find that some people humble their body by lowering their neck and shoulders excessively, but there is no Khushū' in their hearts.

Aisha ؓ saw some youths passing by and they were lowering their shoulders and neck in their walk. She asked her companions: 'Who are these people?' They replied: 'These are al-Nussaak (ascetics).' She ؓ said: 'Umar Ibn al-Khattaab ؓ, when he walked, he was quick; when he spoke, he was heard; if he hit (someone), it would hurt; if he ate, he would eat till satisfied; and indeed he was a truly devout person.' (Madarij Salikeen)

Khushū' is not in lowering your shoulders, or neck, or body: Khushū' is in the heart. You could be walking upright and your heart be filled with Khushū'. On the other hand, you could be lowering your neck and shoulders but your heart is hard as a stone, filled with pride. A person comes to greet with Salaam and he is not responded to or, even worse, the head is nodded. This is not Khushū'. In fact, such Khushū' is a Khushū' of hypocrisy.

Hudayfah ؓ said: beware of Khushū' of hypocrisy. When he was asked what this Khushū' of hypocrisy is, he said, "When the body shows Khushū', but there is no Khushū' in the heart." (Madarij Salikeen)

Hudayfah ؓ said, "The first thing you will lose of your religion will be Khushū' and the last thing you will lose of your religion will be the prayer, and it is well possible that there is no good in a person who prays, and soon will come a time when you shall enter a large Masjid and not see a single person with Khushū'." (Musannaf Ibn Abi Shaybah)

7

P A R A D I S E

E is for . . . Eternal Life

What is causing distractions in your Salah? If I were to tell you to name me five things that are causing you distractions in Salah then what would they be? I can assure you that these would all be related to worldly matters.

Imagine that you are in a very important meeting at work and during the meeting it was the time for Salah, and you want to go and pray Salah. You will be in any one of the following two states:

Either you would pray as though the Salah is extremely heavy and hard on you and it will be difficult for you to leave the meeting and pray. Or you would pray as though the Salah is extremely light and easy for you and it will be easy for you to leave the meeting and pray.

For one who has Khushū', the Salah is light and easy to pray. He does not find it difficult to come out of his meeting, his work or his busy schedule to pray Salah. So how do you get to the level of Khushū' that your Salah becomes light and easy for you for the rest of your life? This is what I am going to share with you in this eighth step in the development of Khushū'. And this step is so important that implementing this step will make your Salah light, which is characteristic of a person with Khushū'.

On the other hand, if you do not implement this step, you will continue to feel the weight of Salah as a burden, which could lead you to distractions in your Salah. Eventually you will continue to pray Salah without Khushū', which is not something I want you to experience.

Reflection on your Death

There is nothing more powerful for making your standing in Salah easy than to think about your death. Because truly the distractions that could be coming your way that are making your Salah a burden on your shoulders, or difficult and hard is related to worldly matters. And when you reflect upon your death and the eternal life (Hereafter) it will make this world and its affairs insignificant before you, which is the cure to this problem. Allah says in the Quran:

وَاسْتَعِينُوا بِالصَّبْرِ وَالصَّلَاةِ ۚ وَإِنَّهَا لَكَبِيرَةٌ إِلَّا عَلَى الْخَاشِعِينَ – الَّذِينَ يَظُنُّونَ أَنَّهُم مُّلَاقُو رَبِّهِمْ وَأَنَّهُمْ إِلَيْهِ رَاجِعُونَ

Seek (Allah's) help with patient perseverance and prayer: it is indeed hard, except to those who are humble.
Who bear in mind the certainty that they are to meet their Lord, and that they are to return to Him. (Quran [1] 2:45-46)

The people who have the most Khushū' are the people who reflect and ponder over their death: they have full faith and certainty that they are going to be meet their Lord. They are constantly pondering upon their grave: this Salah is a radiant light for them in their grave and a means of closeness to Allah. This reflection will develop full Khushū' in your Salah, and you will flee to the Most Merciful, the Most Loving like how the people of Khushū' fled.

Who are the people of Khushū'? Allah says: those who have belief and total certainty that they are to meet their Lord, and they are to return to Him.

In every Salah that you pray, reflect on the fact that you are going to meet Allah and that you are going to return to Him after you die.

If you find it difficult to reflect on your death and on your meeting Allah after you die then my advice to you is to make regular visits to the graveyard. Reflect on your eternal life and meeting Allah by attending funerals (even if it is someone you do not know). The Prophet ﷺ said:

8

كنت نهيتكم عن زيارة القبور ألا فزوروها فإنها تذكركم الآخرة

I used to forbid you to visit graves, but now visit them, for they will remind you of the Hereafter. (Muslim)

Use of these precious times for reflecting and pondering on your death, and your returning to Allah. If at this time you don't reflect, when *will* you reflect?

As you contemplate your death, and as you stand in Salah, you will stand with humbleness and with Khushū', without any distractions, your standing in Salah will become easy for you. Reflect: when you stand before Allah on the Day of Judgement, won't you be humble?

This reflection develops and increases as you remember your death and your return to Allah.

The Road Ahead

I would like to share with you a Hadith of the Prophet ﷺ that I feel contains the essence of this book. In doing so, it is my hope that you will relate to the underlying principles it contains. The Prophet ﷺ said:

أَنْ تَعْبُدَ اللَّهَ كَأَنَّكَ تَرَاهُ ، فَإِنْ لَمْ تَكُنْ تَرَاهُ فَإِنَّهُ يَرَاكَ

To worship Allah as if you see Him, for though you do not see Him, surely He sees you (Muslim)

By following the 8 Steps of 'PARADISE', you will, if Allah wills, get to the level of standing before Allah with the humility, submissiveness and Khushū' which was probably lacking in your Salah until today. You will, by the will of Allah, taste the sweetness in your Salah to the extent that you will be encouraged to pray the night prayers too.

We are in times of temptation all around us, and there is nothing more valuable than your time with Allah the Almighty. Indeed, calling out to Allah and speaking to Allah is a great joy, especially when people are fast asleep. If a servant is truthful to Allah, and begins his night prayer, the dawn may break and he won't even realize that it is the morning due to the sweetness he has felt in his Salah. That's why, when the pious predecessors were asked how some of them were able to recite the entire Quran in one night, they responded, 'By Allah we would begin the night prayer after the Isha Salah and without realising it, by the time of the break of dawn we would have completed the entire Quran.' This was the sweetness of the Quran that no one knows of, except for the one who experiences it.

Night Prayer is the perseverance of the righteous servants of Allah. Those servants who realize the value of this world and the value of the Hereafter. I ask Allah to give me and you this sweetness of the night prayers and may He include us amongst those righteous servants who never missed their night prayers. Ameen.

Next Step

As I conclude this book, my sincere advice to you is that you follow the '8 Steps for developing Khushū' in your Salah' if you really want your Salah to stand out from the masses; because Khushū' is something that is easily lost and is rarely seen, especially in our own times, which are the last times. The Prophet ﷺ said:

أَوَّلُ عِلْمٍ يُرْفَعُ مِنَ النَّاسِ الْخُشُوعُ، يُوشِكُ أَنْ تَدْخُلَ مَسْجِدَ جَمَاعَةٍ فَلَا تَرَى فِيهِ رَجُلًا خَاشِعًا

"The first thing to be lifted up (taken away) from this nation will be khushū', and soon you will enter a large Masjid and not see a single person with khushū'." (Tirmidhi)

I don't want your Salah to be ordinary, I want your Salah to stand out and the only way it will is by implementing the '8 Steps for developing Khushū' in your Salah'. I want you to experience the pleasure, the joy and the happiness that it will bring to your Salah and into your life as a result of following these steps. Very soon a time will come when you will be willing to give up your wealth, property and everything that you possess of this world just for the sake of ONE Sajdah with Khushū'. But it will be too late. Today there is still a chance for you to start to develop this Khushū', while the soul is within you there is still a chance, but no one knows when their final moment is. Don't Delay! Act Now!

I ask Allah the Great, the Lord of the glorious throne, that may He grant us the highest level of Khushū', and that He makes Salah the coolness of our eyes and the warmth of our hearts and the pleasure and joy of our souls. I ask Allah to amend the faults in every Salah that we have prayed until today.

All Praise is due to Allah, the Creator of all, the Giver of everything.

And He is far Exalted above what others ascribe to Him.

And May His Peace and Blessings be upon the

Final Messenger, Prophet Muhammad ﷺ

and all those who follow him.

Ameen

```
┌─────────────┐        ┌─────────────┐        ┌─────────────┐
│ Recitation  │ ◄───── │  Awareness  │ ◄───── │ Preparation │
└─────────────┘        └─────────────┘        └─────────────┘
```

Preparation

- Wudhu → Recall the virtues of Wudhu
- Walking to Salah → Recall the virtues of walking to Salah
- Secret of 'Allahu Akbar' → As you raise your hands, throw everything related to this world behind you

Awareness

- Greatness of Salah → Recall the magnificence and the greatness of Salah
- Greatness of Allah
  - Know who Allah is through His Names and Attributes
  - Reflect on Allah's blessings
- Enmity of Shaitan and Friendship of → Know Shaitan is your enemy. Allah, His messengers, and the believers are your true friends

Recitation

- Reflect over Recitation
  - Pause at end of each Ayah
  - Reflect over the meaning of your recitation
  - Reflect over the response from Allah
- Cry over Recitation
  - Recall the virtues of weeping
  - Listen to moving speeches and lectures

168

An Overview of the 8 Steps of Actions

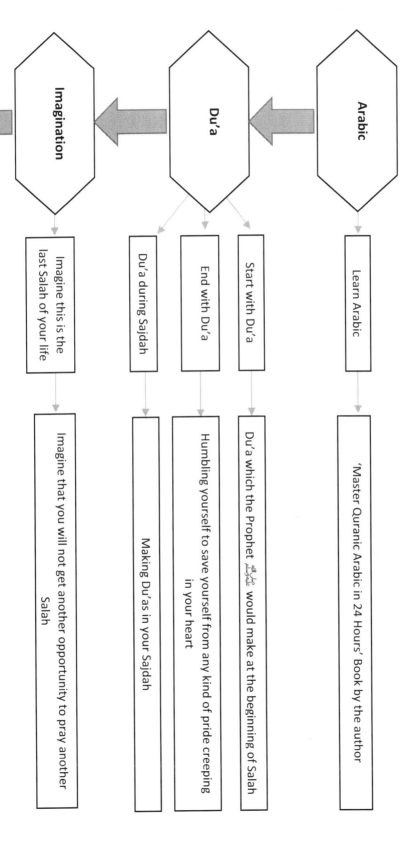

Arabic

Learn Arabic

'Master Quranic Arabic in 24 Hours' Book by the author

Du'a

Start with Du'a

Du'a which the Prophet ﷺ would make at the beginning of Salah

End with Du'a

Humbling yourself to save yourself from any kind of pride creeping in your heart

Du'a during Sajdah

Making Du'as in your Sajdah

Imagination

Imagine this is the last Salah of your life

Imagine that you will not get another opportunity to pray another Salah

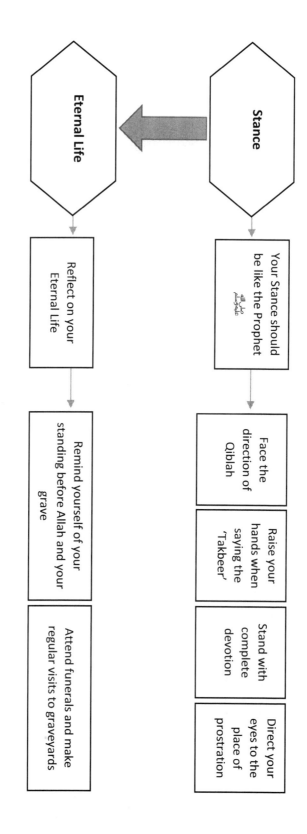

Stance

→ **Eternal Life**

Your Stance should be like the Prophet صلى الله عليه وسلم

- Face the direction of Qiblah
- Raise your hands when saying the 'Takbeer'
- Stand with complete devotion
- Direct your eyes to the place of prostration

Reflect on your Eternal Life

- Remind yourself of your standing before Allah and your grave
- Attend funerals and make regular visits to graveyards

Bibliography

The Holy Quran [1] trans Yusuf Ali

The Holy Quran [2] trans Mufti Taqi Usmani

The Holy Quran [3] trans Dr. Mohsin

Abu Talha Muhammed Yunus Ibn Abd Sattat, (1420) Aynal Khashioona Fis Salah, Al Waheed, Makkah

Ibn Al Qayyim, (2009), Mdarijus Salikeen [Volume 1] Dar al-kotob Al-ilmiyah, Lebanon

Sad Ibn Ali Qahtani (1430) Al Khushoo Fi Salah Fi Zawil Kitaab Wa Sunnah

Shaykh Muhammad Saalih al-Munajjid, 33 Sababan Lil Khushooe Fi Salah

Shaykh Muhammad Saalih al-Munajjid (2015) Islamqa.info [Online] Available from: http://islamqa.info/en/ (Last Accessed on 20th January 2015)

Shaykh Shinqitee (n.d) [Audio Cassettes] Riyadh